IN THE WAKE OF WAR

Eight million Frenchmen served in the Great War. This ground-breaking study examines their politics and social situation within French society in the interwar years. The author provides the authoritative account of the veterans and their associations, which spanned the gamut of French politics. Above all he shows conclusively that veterans' patriotism, while profoundly held, was an expression of their commitment to civic rather than military virtues and values. Indeed the didactic, pacifist intent of much of their commemorative and public work in the interwar period distinguishes their outlook and aspirations from those of most other European veterans' organisations. The author has prepared a new introduction especially for this English edition.

Antoine Prost is Professor of History at the University of Paris, I.

THE LEGACY OF THE GREAT WAR
A series sponsored by the Historial de la grande guerre Péronne-Somme

General Editor
JAY WINTER

F o r t h c o m i n g

Rosa Maria Bracco
MERCHANTS OF HOPE
British Middlebrow Writers and the First World War, 1919–1939

Patrick Fridenson
THE FRENCH HOME FRONT 1914–1918

Stéphane Audoin-Rouzeau
MEN AT WAR 1914–1918

Gerald D. Feldman
ARMY, INDUSTRY, AND LABOR IN GERMANY 1914–1918

IN THE WAKE OF WAR

'Les Anciens Combattants' and French Society

ANTOINE PROST

Translated by
HELEN McPHAIL

BERG
PROVIDENCE / OXFORD

English edition
first published in 1992 by
Berg Publishers Limited
Editorial offices:
165 Taber Avenue, Providence, RI 02906, USA
150 Cowley Road, Oxford, OX4 1JJ, UK

Published with the support of the French Ministry of Culture

English edition © 1992
Originally published as *Les anciens combattants et la société française*.
Translated from the French by permission of the publishers
Gallimard, Paris.

A CIP catalogue record for this book is available from the British Library.

Library of Congress Cataloging-in-Publication Data
Prost, Antoine, 1933–
[Anciens combattants et la société française. English]
In the wake of war : les anciens combattants and French society /
p. cm. — (The Legacy of the Great War)
Translation of: Les anciens combattants et la société française.
Includes index.
ISBN 0–85496–672–2. — ISBN 0–85496–337–5 (pbk.)
1. World War, 1914–1918—Veterans—France. 2. Veterans—France—
Political activity—History—20th century. 4. France—Social
conditions—20th century. I. Title. II. Series.
940.4' 1244—dc20 92-13236
CIP
ISBN 0–85496–672–2
ISBN 0–85496–337–5 (pbk.)

Printed in Great Britain by
Billing and Sons Ltd, Worcester

CONTENTS

ABBREVIATIONS

AGMG   Association générale des mutilés de la guerre (General Association of War-Disabled Men)

ARAC   Association républicaine des anciens combattants (Republican Association of Veterans)

FN   Fédération nationale des Associations françaises de mutilés, réformés et veuves de guerre (Fédération Maginot) (National Federation of French Associations of Disabled and Discharged Men and War Widows - the Magino Federation)

FNAPG   Fédération nationale des anciens prisonniers de guerre (National Federation of Former Prisoners of War)

FNBPC   Fédération nationale des blessés du poumon et chirurgicaux (National Federation of Sufferers from Lung and Surgical Wounds)

FNCR   Fédération nationale des combattants républicains (National Federation of Republican Servicemen)

FDP   Fédération ouvrière et paysanne (Workers' and Peasants' Federation)

SDC   Semaine du combattant (The Serviceman's Week)

UF   Union Fédérale (Federal Union)

UNC   Union nationale des combattants (National Union of Servicemen)

UNMR   Union nationale des mutilés et réformés (National Union of Disabled and Discharged Men)

Preface to the English Edition

The French words 'anciens combattants' have been translated here as 'veterans', but, as the reader will notice, the English phrase does not have the same echoes as does the French. We ought to reflect on the fact that when one word has no equivalent in another language, it generally suggests that we confront one of the particularities of a given society. Such is precisely the case with the word 'veterans'.

After the war, many men who had been involved in this huge and dreadful conflict created societies of a specific kind. They came together for mourning, for commemoration, for mutual help, for friendly meetings, and to put pressure on public opinion for an improvement of their own rights, to make sure that the massacre would not be forgotten and that war would not burst out again. These societies had periodic meetings and formal ceremonies, they had branches in most villages, even the smallest, and their membership exceeded three million in the early 1930s. This was not a small epiphenomenon of some antiquarian type.

When looking at this book, fifteen years after its first publication, it seems to me that it presents three points of interest. Obviously, the first is related to the long-lasting damage of the war. Throughout their lives, these men were marked by the war. They never forgot it. It is impossible to understand fully what this war was, without looking at these enduring consequences. These people refused even to imagine that a new war would come; they did not disavow the soldiers they had been they would not say anything against patriotism, but they desperately sought to avoid the emergence of a second Franco-German confrontation. They were deeply pacifist. This book tries to explore this curious mixture of shrewd thinking, commitment and illusion, rooted in the common ground of Republican primary education and the memory of the war, which brought them to associate patriotism and pacifism. The political history of France between the wars is impenetrable without taking into account this collective background.

The second interesting feature is the importance of voluntary associations in French society. Some American political scientists have stressed the weakness of French associative life, and they have found in this supposed lack of associations one reason for the strength of a highly centralised and overpowerful state. I cannot agree with this interpretation. Associations such as veterans' societies were – and still are – numerous, as any junior politician knows. The story of the veterans' societies demonstrates, on the contrary, the strength and activity of associations in France. Further, it shows how the very ideal of association was praised by these former pupils of the Republican primary school. They respected legal and formal procedures; they carefully kept the minutes of their meetings; they solemnly held their general assemblies and elected their officials. Association was for them not only a means of lobbying parliament or helping themselves: it was also a right granted by the Republic. Creating societies was dignified as one of the privileges of the Citizen.

Here, we are close to the third interest of this story, which is its character as a kind of ethnological survey of French society. When scrutinising these associations, we look at one major part of French society, that of the villages and small towns, which still constituted the core of the nation on the eve of the Second World War. Hence the attention given to what these leaders said: rather than expressing opinions or ideas, their stereotypes refer to a set of deeply rooted attitudes. We tried not to separate what was said from who was speaking or writing, and in what context. Historians should not try to interpret statements without considering the whole social framework: otherwise, anybody could be deemed a fascist or a bolshevik. This kind of disembodied history would be too easy and misleading. We have considered even apparently meaningless addresses not as the dotages of silly people, but as data of which the historian has to elucidate the meaning. Hence the importance given, in this book, both to quotations and to the texture of the language.

This particularity has made the translation of the book a very difficult undertaking. I would like to conclude this preface by saying how grateful I am to Helen McPhail, who translated this rather untranslatable literature, and to Jay Winter, who suggested the undertaking and carefully edited this book with warmth, friendliness and rigorous attention.

ANTOINE PROST
Pembroke College,
Cambridge, 5 December 1991

Introduction

It cannot be said that the veterans of the 1914–1918 war had any significant impact on political life in the interwar years: the history of the period can be written without mentioning them more than a few times, with reference to a demonstration for which they turned out in strength. Their importance for us is not as actors but as witnesses. Their responses, their opinions, their behaviour as a body, the fact that they existed at all, are evidence of the traumas of the Great War. They revealed too the mentality and attitudes that were widespread among the French in the 1930s. Within the society of that period they were an enduring reminder of unprecedented slaughter – but also of forms of social interaction, moral and political beliefs, patterns of life which seemed natural.

I have spent some years studying veterans, organizations, their demonstrations and their publications. Like all research, it was often wearisome, but at times it was also moving, and my experience of these men convinced me of the significance of their movement. It also enlightened me: the reality of the fighting soldier was vastly different from the image usually presented. This had nothing to do with military spirit, with factions, or with fascism. It is primarily because it was a mass movement, with more than three million members: the 1914 war was the whole nation under arms, and the veterans represented the whole nation. They included among their number a few authoritarian reactionaries and a few revolutionaries, but, as in the nation as a whole, the vast majority were peace-loving, patriotic and republican.

This book has been written, therefore, rather as an archaeologist might uncover a great city buried under the sand, to bring to light the wealth and diversity of its former life where passers-by now see only a simple signpost. Too many people are convinced that veterans mean right-wing propagandists; but the former were quiet retiring provincials while the latter understood the uses of publicity. I therefore intend to address first those aspects of the veterans' movement that are neglected in popular thinking – but I will do my best not to replace one simplistic notion with another. In these brief pages it would be impossible to tell the whole story, nor yet to prove everything, and the reader may occasionally feel that I demand to be taken at face value. The reader may be reassured: anyone who is dissatisfied or sceptical may find fuller arguments in the thesis which I have published elsewhere.[1]

I will take as my point of departure the soldiers' enduring memories of their war, as a context for the outline of the inception and nature of their associations which follows. Then I will attempt to assess what the veterans did when they met for a day together. This analysis should make it possible to establish more clearly the veterans' attitudes towards their country, the army, the peace, and politics.

---

1. Antoine Prost, *Les Anciens Combattants et la société française, 1914–1939,* 3 vols., Paris, Presses de la Fondation nationale des Sciences politiques, 1977.

1

Recollection

How did the soldiers of 1914–18 remember their war? Which episodes left an abiding impression? How much of the war remained in their memories, in 1930 or in 1940?

The Experience of Death

To have risked your life is nothing – practically every car driver has narrowly avoided road accidents without suffering long-term anxieties. What leaves a deep impression is the sight of death at close quarters.[1] It is the overwhelming and inescapable presence of one's own imminent death. Front-line soldiers spent whole days, often whole weeks, in close familiarity or intimacy with death: a permanent threat, an image visibly present on all sides, an emotion impossible to dominate completely, because it undermines simultaneously human reasoning, feelings and innermost instincts. The front-line soldier's experience was centred around this continual pulsating presence of death,

> . . . of a death which ceased to be accepted as a concept, but was instead, suddenly and unremittingly, a presence as real as, for example, that of a hornet buzzing around your head, which flies away briefly, then returns, making your skin crawl in revulsion with the brush of its wings, and which at any second may sting you, must surely sting you.[2]

The experience of mass death in war is an extraordinary and unforgettable revelation that leaves no individual unchanged. It is impossible to continue afterwards as though it had never happened. The front was a vast charnel-house and the soldiers lived among corpses. All war memoirs, without exception, include macabre anecdotes.

The least disturbing tell of ancient remains, of dry bones blending into the earth itself until a tibia looked like a bit of wood and could be used as a hook for a haversack. The men made efforts to bury or

Notes to Chapter 1 can be found on page 25.

3

remove the bodies of their comrades killed in the trenches; but many corpses lay between the lines. One could not always avoid seeing them by a casual glance over the parapet, and the stale smell of them, a 'flat, cold, bitter stink',[3] was a reminder of their presence. The most striking discoveries, however, awaited the soldiers as they went up the line or back down from the front, along trenches under artillery observation, thoroughfares where only stretcher-bearers with time to spare did anything about dead bodies. In such places relieving troops found appalling sights, corpses piled up on top of each other at the most dangerous points, bloody fragments, a greatcoat caught on a tree-stump.

> That's where I saw . . . three dead soldiers, doubtless killed by the same shell; their bodies were part of an indeterminate bloody mass; that's a sight which I have never forgotten,

noted an eye-witness in 1964. Another recalled his reactions and those of his companions at the same period, when faced with a similar sight:

> No matter how hardened the men who saw death all around them in all its forms, they would turn their eyes away. Without speaking. It was only much further on that you would hear someone say, as if to himself, 'That wasn't a very nice sight, for God's sake. . . .'[4]

Even worse, perhaps, was the physical contact during night relief operations, with a corpse to be stepped around or over, or those muddy communication trenches where sometimes you would step on something soft and yielding which was a dead body. 'Oh, if our poor wives could see us now!' someone would shout in a rough tense voice (one of Francisque Vial's territorials),[5] while sometimes the young recruits would be unable to stop themselves vomiting.[6]

There is no need to plunge into neo-realistic descriptions of terrible charnel-houses, à la Barbusse. Commanding officers tried to keep them from their men's eyes and few witnessed, as did André Ducasse, territorials using pitchforks to unload carts full of corpses.[7] On the other hand it was a terrible mistake on the part of the staff officers to keep on sending soldiers back into the same lines, where the bodies they found were those of their comrades, friends whom they recognised, with whom they had shared bread, wine and tobacco. Going up the line the hero of *La Percée* saw in this way the corpses of men from his own regiment:

> Favigny and the group of friends could easily make out the dark blue cloth of their capes, the dark blue or purple-tinged fabric of their képi-covers, and they knew it well. They thought of themselves in the place of these dead men. Obviously, soon they would all be just like them.[8]

As Maurice Genevoix confirmed, half a century later,

> Rediscovering at each successive relief the same poor wretched things was undoubtedly worse, in absolute terms, than having to face up to danger yet again. It meant suffering the overwhelming impression of being condemned to death without any hope of mercy.[9]

Then there were the interminable death throes witnessed by soldiers as brothers and impotent spectators. To see a trench companion suffering, shouting, calling, sobbing, or simply gazing silently, as if imploring the help which no one could offer, receiving last confidential requests, heartbreaking in their simplicity – all this was intolerable. No one could forget such moments. In 1964 a farm worker from the Lot, one of the millions of soldiers in the ranks, an eyewitness of minimal education, still remembered the death of an officer in his arms:

> Many, many times I've heard his cries in my nightmares, and my great sorrow is that I was not able to carry out his last wishes.[10]

In other ways, ordinary soldiers were present as spectators, distressed but even less able to help, at the death of innumerable anonymous men whose cries and dying gasps sought their help in vain. One account may stand for many more; it too comes from an ordinary soldier, whose lack of education is apparent in the original spelling and punctuation:

> What I found most terrible and most demoralising during the war when there was attack and counterattack, that is advance and retreat at night keeping guard in a shell hole when there was a minute or two of calm and silence, it was terrible to hear the wounded of both sides crying out screaming and on quiet nights you could hear it a long way off and no way to relieve them unless they were very close – our job was to watch and listen. After moments of quiet the groaning began again far off and came closer, explosions machine-gun fire that often finished off the wounded all the noise covered the cries of the dying.
>
> You have to have been there to understand what it means to hear these cries of all kinds it was demoralising and a night was a very long time in such conditions and you would think that tomorrow it would be your turn. I can't find words strong enough to describe a night on guard on a battlefield where there had been an advance and a retreat during the day.[11]

Sympathy could not be separated from a more intimately felt distress. As one soldier expressed it, 'However much of a man you may be, when you see friends all round you with mortal wounds, you say to yourself: it'll soon be my turn'.[12] The death of others was a constant reminder of one's own mortality, and that is what constituted the very essence of this unforgettable experience.

Fear

Anguish was particularly severe in attack and under shelling. In some respects the actual attack came as a relief. Only one thing mattered: getting to the opposite trench, what Gabriel Chevallier called the stampede of the attack:

> Standing up in the open. The sudden feeling of nakedness, of being unprotected. . . .
>
> Our lives at stake! A sort of oblivion. . . .
>
> Only the immediate details of the terrain are noticed, and the simple action of running absorbs all our faculties.
>
> Men fall, split open, scatter in pieces. Shots miss us. . . . We hear the noise of other men being hit, their strangled cries. Every man for himself. We run, surrounded. Fear operates now like a spring, releasing animal strength, blotting out emotions.
>
> A machine-gun fires exasperatingly, on the left. Where to go? Forward! That's where it's safe. We attack in order to find shelter.[13]

Waiting for the attack, on the other hand, was an endless and testing time. As soon as they knew they were to attack, the soldiers felt the threat of death hovering over them. Preparations forced them into activity which helped to prevent thought, but there are things which are terribly hard to do, when you think that it may be for the last time: changing your underwear, for example.

> No one would commit the sacrilege of talking at this time. This preparation of men condemned to death before the sentence of capital punishment was carried out was painful. Suddenly I wanted to cry, and I escaped into the stairway to smother my sobs.[14]

Men wrote to their families, with an intensity which had to be restrained so as not to alarm them, but trying to pass on to them the full extent of their tender feelings. A stifled silence reigned, barely broken by a few angry exclamations. Then it was time to go up the line, always in that heavy silence, *a silence of human anguish broken by ripples . . . of swearing.*[15] The real waiting began in the jumping-off trenches, when there was nothing to do but count the minutes until the fateful hour. The distribution of spirits on such occasions did not stop men thinking:

> There they are, pale, their faces drawn, hardened by many sleepless nights; their ill-shaven faces seem marked by something overwhelmingly powerful.
>
> The most light-hearted men are solemn and silent now, the most hardened turn in on themselves; all look withdrawn in their efforts to dominate the fear which they have mastered so often before.[16]

This is very different from soldiers impatient to use their bayonets, the cliché foot-sloggers of patriotic imaginings, unaware of the true scale of their situation. The truth was more moving and more human. An officer commented on it during the war:

> How much more I love the men I have seen half an hour before the attack, pale and silent, their eyes fixed, lying at the bottom of the jumping-off trench, a tragic line of frightened faces.[17]

Each man struggled in vain to find strength within himself, in his recollections, his hopes, his faith. Many prayed silently and no one, even the most convinced agnostic, dreamed of mocking them: but in the immobility of waiting all throats were knotted tight with anguish until the unleashing of attack released them.

Action was indeed the best way – the only way – to eliminate such distress, and this is what made artillery bombardment so testing. The soldiers were submitted to indiscriminate shelling without any possibility of turning their fear to action. Waiting for an attack had a known limit, and distress increased until the inexorable zero hour; but the experience of being shelled was very different – it was endless, there was no fixed time limit. In the major battles of the war shells fell continuously for days on end: the sight of companions being killed was convincing proof that the ordeal would not end until all the trench's occupants were dead. There was nothing to be done, except submit and wait for death. This, in the true sense, was martyrdom, it was, indeed, a 'Passion'.

It is difficult to recreate in a few pages a visceral fear endured for endless hours. Gabriel Chevallier attempted it in *La Peur*, but I find his narrative a little laboured; the passages at the core of Maurice Genevoix's *Les Eparges* seem to me – and this is also the opinion of that ruthless critic-witness Jean Norton Cru[18] – more truthful and more authentic. A lengthy quotation is permissible; no other war book can equal these pages:

> Once only, that night, we felt the same surge of panic, the same sharp jolt of the heart: a shell had just exploded close to us; and, as we began to raise our heads after it, we were terrified by fierce sizzling. Richomme and Bouaré bellowed in the darkness. Then we laughed as we realised it was a lost flare, shooting off sideways in a great hiss of sparks.
>
> After that they were all the same. I remained leaning against the side of the trench with a puddle of yellow water between my feet. Propped against me, on my left, Lardin moulded himself into the mud with the pressure of his body; on my right, Bouaré's shoulder pressed gently against me. . . .

Bouaré, Lardin, and I were in the midst of falling shells. We ended up imagining shells falling for all eternity. Our imagination and feelings were not up to the scale of such bombardment, not ready. It would come. We were really there. When one of us risked a movement, there would be a little damp noise as he shifted; when a shell whistled closer we shrank back further into ourselves, and breathed more easily after it burst. We lost all idea of time: the sky above us remained calmly grey between the two banks of clay; from time to time a little cold rain spread icy ripples over them and the yellow puddle shimmered between my feet.

Sometimes, when I had to, I stood up. That was rare: even when a shell fell into crater number 7 and human remains burst up black against the sky, unavoidably recognisable as an arm, a leg or a head, I stuck to the soft and slippery mould of mud gradually shaped by my body. But when a shell landed without whistling in the platoon's trench, I stood up. That felt better, even if it was useless. I saw Legallais' back, stripped bare and white round an enormous wound which continued to palpitate, and as I looked at this wound I calculated what one could 'get into' it. . . .

We looked at the trembling puddle of water, the banks of earth, the one particular place of all places where a shell was bound to fall. 'But it's really happening. . . .' That is what we believed. Increasingly often, as we became more weary, feverish images were thrown up among the shell bursts: of jumping up with our bodies in fragments; of falling back onto the parapet with broken backs, like Legallais; of being headless, our heads torn off in a single blow, like Grondin, or Mémasse, or Libron, whose head came rolling down to us. . . .

There was no respite; each of us could feel his stomach cramped as if by a steady hard grasp. Against my shoulder Bouaré's shoulder began to tremble gently, continuously.

Then night fell, without any break in the shelling, and the dawn of the fourth day broke over Les Eparges:

> A great shaking of earth and heaven across scorching eyelids; damp chill; rediscovering things in the pale dawn, one after another, everything: no one killed in the darkness, no one even buried despite the ferocious shelling; the same earth, the same corpses; flesh quivering with inner twitching, leaping, deep and warm, and painful; no more images, even, just the burning fatigue frozen by the rain on the skin; day returning to the ridge while all the Boche batteries continued to fire on it, on what remained of us up there, mixed with blood and bodies, with the soil that was once so fertile, contaminated now with poisons, with dead flesh, beyond cleansing of our foul ordeal.
>
> Are they going to counterattack again? They are simply firing at us: it's cowardly.

Porchon, Maurice Genevoix's friend, was killed that morning. At the time he scarcely reacted.

It was only long afterwards that I grasped it, in the hollow of damp clay where I went to sit down between Lardin and Bouaré: a hard chill, a disgusted indifference towards everything that I could see, the indignity of the mud and the wretchedness of the dead bodies, the dreary day on the ridge, the savagery of the shells. . . . I was no longer even conscious of my fatigue: I was no longer afraid of anything, not even of my bones being crushed beneath one of those great falls, nor of my flesh tearing in the bite of bursting steel. I no longer felt sorry for the living, not Bouaré who was trembling, nor Lardin lying flat, nor myself. No violence surged up within me, no wave of grief, no flash of manly indignation. It was not even despair, this shrivelling in my heart that I could taste in my throat; nor resignation either. . . . Only this: a hard chill, dried-out indifference, like a shrivelling of the soul. . . . Meaning? It is without meaning. The world, on the ridge of Les Eparges, the whole world was dancing through time, a kind of insane farce, whirling around me in hideous flickerings, incomprehensible, grotesque. . . .

That was when the 210 mm shell fell. I felt it simultaneously on the back of my neck, a heavy bludgeoning blow, and in front of me, a red and growling blast. That is how a shell kills you.

The shell killed Lardin and Bouaré; Genevoix survived '*absurdly*'. The torture continued through the day, and the next day. 'Oh you poor . . . poor boys!' – the heartfelt greeting of their landlady on their return to Belrupt in the middle of the night was the only possible response to such an ordeal. It was the response of the *mater dolorosa* receiving the body from the Cross: the comparison was made by an eyewitness in 1964, responding to Roger Boutefeu's survey on a picture postcard showing Our Lady of Sorrows by Simon Marmion in Strasbourg museum:

> The war holds no jaunty military memories for me; for me it is only the ultimate symbol of cruelty and human stupidity unleashed in collective madness.
>
> Why otherwise would I write to you on any picture but this desolate woman, plunged in inconsolable grief by the consequences of war.[19]

The deepest understanding of the war is perhaps that of the artist Rouault, inspired by it to create his *Miserere* engravings.

Causing Death

This experience of death constituted a kind of voyage to the end of night which made an enduring impression on soldiers. It was not however the only impression. Some men killed, and this particular experience was no less heavy to bear for being pushed into the darkest recesses of consciousness, although many soldiers never killed a single enemy soldier. Artillery soldiers and most of the territorial army had virtually no direct contact with the enemy. Even among the front-line infantry soldiers, how many fired only at random on a vaguely-seen group of the enemy? How many never knew that it was their bullet which brought down a particular opponent? Some certainly felt the full knowledge of having killed: they saw their enemy fall, they picked them out among others, and they were near enough when they killed them to hear them cry out or perceive their expression. They were only a minority, no doubt, but a not inconsiderable minority, and even if it was unusual, combat at close quarters unfortunately did occur. It was not like the descriptions of unconsciously sadistic imaginings, and bayonets proved more cumbersome than practical, but it was not fiction, and no one forgot that he had killed.

Maurice Genevoix, for example, killed two or three Germans in a night encounter in September 1914. In 1960 he recalled this episode. He had not seen the men at whom he fired his revolver. On the other hand:

> The two cries, so alike, that I still hear them after more than 40 years, I genuinely heard them that night at La Vaux-Marie.[20]

A single detail reveals how deeply this memory impressed the writer: in the first edition of *Sous Verdun* he recounted the episode and commented: 'they fell with the same strangled cry'; but in later editions he personally censored the passage and only restored it in 1950: 'feeling it was dishonest to omit deliberately one of the incidents of the war which most deeply disturbed me, and of which the scar has never faded from my memory.'

To have killed left a guilty memory. Most eyewitness accounts include an attempt at justification: 'that's war', or, 'it was unavoidable', as if there was no end to self-reproach. Here is just one example, from a young soldier:

> As we reached the top five or six wretched soldiers, stupefied by the pounding fire, emerged out of their hole in front of me. In the confusion of action I could not see that they were unarmed and were putting their hands up. I was startled despite everything, for I was alone and separated from my companions, and in an uncontrollable reflex my finger pressed the trigger and shot one of the poor wretches full in the chest. He was unarmed, and was surrendering. Ignoring his companions, who scurried off down the slopes to save their lives, I bent over him as if to seek forgiveness. I do not know whether there was reproach in his gaze. I did not dare look into his

dying eyes. With his hand clenched over the hole in his chest he tried to stop the blood spurting out. He was still sufficiently conscious to get his wallet out of the inside pocket of his tunic, and hold it out to me. I opened it quickly and found photographs. A very young wife, two young children. I understood his gesture and the wish it expressed. I made him understand that the photos would be sent back to his family. His eyes thanked me. I could already see the shadow of death across his face. I held my water bottle to his lips, and with a final twitch he died in my arms.

I have often seen the ghost of this dead man since then. I reject the responsibility for my deeds, I hand it over to others, for as an 18-year-old soldier I should have had other examples to follow. Alas, it is only human beings, whoever they may be, who can make war with a spirit of humanity.[21]

It is unnatural to fire at another human being, and no one who did it could avoid feeling guilty. Even if remorse is not explicit in the self-reproaches of those who fought in the war, there is always the awareness of having transgressed a basic interdiction. War is barbarous in its daily reality: massacre, carnage, butchery. It is barbarous precisely because it constrains men to infringe a fundamental principle of every culture: 'Thou shalt not kill'. It matters little, therefore, if some soldiers did or did not experience some kind of primitive pleasure in killing, as some maintain, adding yet more to the horror of war, or whether they simply did their duty: the task itself was guilty. Repugnance felt about war is not only the rejection of a terrible anguish: it is also a moral protest.

The Softening of Recollection

The fundamental fear of killing and being killed, in its anguish and compassion as in its remorse, is not one that can be communicated. It marks the soldier and sets him apart from other men. They were soon aware of this. 'I was dedicated, among dedicated men', recalled Maurice Genevoix.[22] Jean Bernier warned: 'He who has not understood physically is incapable of telling you about it. You, the people who read what I say, you cannot understand',[23] and Jean Norton Cru echoes him: 'It was in our flesh that we understood the war'.[24] No description, no matter how heartfelt, could match the emotional intensity of such an experience. Even when we manage to arouse our own emotions – which is essential – at the thought of what the war meant for those who took part in it, we remain irredeemably ignorant of the spirit and the inner misgivings that gave this experience, at the time, its richness and power. For those who fought, the memory could not be dissociated from a sort of physical disturbance. Half a century later they were still seized with emotion when they evoked their memories:

> For a long time afterwards I went on reliving that terrible and long-drawn-out martyrdom, with sweat on my brow. Still today my brow is moist and my heart full of bitterness as I finish telling you about it.[25]

Thus the dimming of memories – which was relative – was a slow process. During the war and the immediate postwar period the experience of death was too close to be recalled. The combatants did not talk about it. Norton Cru was surprised at Dorgelès and Barbusse: how could they have passed over in silence 'that which was most terrible in a soldier's life?'[26] In fact all the books written 'in the heat of the moment' are silent on the soldier's anguish. They emphasise the profound difference separating combatant troops from those who took no part in the war, without describing the most important experience. Indeed they felt it was an impossible undertaking. They despaired of being able to make others understand what they had lived through. But there was also genuine modesty: the experience was too intimate to be spoken of lightly. It was all right to talk about hunger, cold, mud, rats, or lice, but not of matters as personal as anguish: 'material miseries were the only ones that he [the soldier] could decently admit to'.[27] Above all, the soldiers were the prisoners of civilian expectations: they could only say what civilians allowed them to say. Lies or silence became the only alternative. They lied sometimes for the wrong reasons: to flatter the militaristic patriotism which turned them into heroes. Georges Scott, the artist who provided the magazine *L'Illustration* with so many heroic cover designs, wrote for example to Barbusse: 'this is only picture-making. You will see that what I am doing for myself, for afterwards, is very different'.[28] All the war narratives evoke this conflict in the classic episode of men on leave: what the *poilus* had to say fitted so ill with what was expected of them that many lied to please those who thought of them as heroes and were always ready to argue with them:

> To all the betrayals we have already made for the war we must add the betrayal of our honesty. Since our sacrifice cannot be accurately valued we feed the legend, with derisive laughter.[29]

But there were other good reasons for lying: the wish to reassure one's nearest and dearest. Alain complains of this to his former pupils:

> I have read many of those letters described as 'admirable', admirable in one sense; some sent to me by well-loved young friends, and all killed, or nearly all. . . .

You have outrun fate, gathering your manly strength and creating a fine figure of innocence condemned and marching to execution. But why should you wish to console me in particular? Why didn't you tell me finally that you loved life and that it was hard for you to give it up. Everyone should have been allowed this reproach. 'My God, my God, why hast thou forsaken me?' You should have been a bit hard, and stuck to the truth first of all. And perhaps you have no right to console through lying, even to the women. This lie may kill another million young men within ten years.[30]

It took about ten years for memories to settle, and for the soldiers to begin evoking their war. They did so first through the most superficial aspects, the most anecdotal. It was only in 1931 that the most influential veterans' journal opened its columns to descriptions of war, for items without strong emotion, evoking rats, lice, or the rough wine.[31] In that same year Alain began writing his memoirs, recounting things 'less strictly, less severely, in the course of the narrative, and primarily for my own pleasure'.[32] At the same time André Bridoux published his *Souvenirs du temps des morts*. In it he observed:

For the soldier, peace was long in coming, for the discord in his mind survived the war. . . . On coming out of the army, life received him ill, and this return to civilian life, so much longed for in hours of danger, was a source of fresh disappointment, sometimes of bitterness and despair; to earn his living he had to apply himself to tedious trades, with the very painful feeling that he was seen as an importunate ghost. Life went on, however, and ten years had passed; a period fully necessary for thoughts to begin to clarify.[33]

The finest account of this slow sifting of memories is that of Maurice Genevoix, in a book published in a limited edition with an enigmatic title for all but veterans: *H.O.E*, for *Hopitaux d'opération et d'évacuation*. In this he described his own rehabilitation to civilian life through conversation resumed between two friends at the end of a school's ceremonial dinner for its former pupils. For the first time at such an event, it fell to a veteran to make the after-dinner speech. Genevoix spoke in a familiar way to one of the guests, recalling the guest's astonishment when they met again. He had been struck by Genevoix's soberness, his restraint, 'a strange secret modesty, not in the least disdainful, yet which gave his speech a somewhat stiff or chilly air. . . . Is it true, you hoped for more warmth and relaxation? . . . Is it my fault if I feel with such poignant force that such realities remain incomprehensible for those who have not lived through them?'

While he was speaking, the former pupils who were in the war felt closer to each other. But Genevoix observes:

A few years earlier, at the time when this shock hit us, as sharp and brutal as the weight of a chain, we would have felt our isolation. Brought closer together, and cut off, at the same time: separate from all the men who had not for an interminable moment had their lives tossed into that hell, into that nightmare of filth and blood. . . .

Today, for the first time, my undimmed feelings have left me, here among you all. They have lost that flavour of overwhelming helplessness, that weight of despair which was an inescapable part of it.

After the dinner Genevoix told his friend about his life since leaving hospital. He concludes:

Ten years, my friends. . . . It took you ten years to understand – at what terrible cost – that the war was really over. And that was peace, for this man, and this man, for each one in his fresh misery, in his poor man's loneliness. Ten years, my friend, is quite a quick cure. Despite it we will have worked, survived, bravely rejoined our own age.[34]

The calm which thus appears to heal over the scars after about a decade did not make the veterans any more inclined to talk about what impressed them during the war. Certainly there were some chatterers, but they were rare: discretion was far more widespread. Some even reproach them for it, like this young girl, a war orphan, who presented a report on youth to the Union Fédérale congress in 1930.* In her eyes the veterans were responsible for a misunderstanding between them and the younger generation:

The veterans have done nothing to help us understand their life during the war years. They cut out of their lives those years which remind them only of hardships or, when they recall them, they avoid all painful details.[35]

On the other hand the settling of memories made it possible for veterans to take stock of their lives. With the distance of time, they became more aware of how the war had changed them.

The Personal Challenge

The first emotion to appear was pride. A modest pride, but confident. Being in the war was a trial, in both senses of the word: a crisis, but also a judgement. Jean Guéhenno expressed it well: 'The true drama took place within one's own mind. . . . It was impossible for us not to know how we stood in the face of death'.[36]

*The UF or Union Fédérale was the largest federation of veterans' societies, with more than 900,000 members (see chapter 2). The UF had created a branch of 'UF's youth', which affiliated sons and daughters of its members. This young girl was speaking on behalf of that branch.

Overall, it was a positive experience. Most soldiers came out of it strengthened. An eyewitness expressed it simply, in 1964:

Gentlemen,

It is with no great pleasure that I respond to the appeal in your columns, for the memories of the past are often still painful despite the modest pride that they offer.[37]

This 'modest pride' was no vainglorious militarism, no collective arrogance, no vanity at belonging to a victorious army or nation. It was an entirely personal feeling, something intimate, an inner confidence, an esteem which one could bestow on oneself. Veterans knew now that they were not cowards. They did not think of themselves as heroes, and they would gladly have been spared the ordeal; but, after all, they had had this unique experience and had not failed to rise to it. André Bridoux observed this accurately:

The worst of experiences leave no resentment against life if one has found the courage to hold on. Much more than that, one is always content with the memory of something in the past at which one has not flinched. . . .

Thus the quality of our memories is linked to the qualities of spirit which we have demonstrated in the process of acquiring those memories, and the greatest benefit of courage is undoubtedly to prepare us for the pleasure of recollecting them in the future.

Hence a conflict, almost dramatic in tone, in the mind of the survivor,

between his intellect which resists the very concept of revisiting the trials of war, and his memory, in which these trials, far from appearing dreadful, become increasingly dear to him in their reflection of the valiance and youth needed to overcome them.[38]

This is the way to understand the apparent contradiction of veterans who tirelessly recall the horror of war, and yet sometiems evoke it or talk about it with a kind of tenderness. Their burden was too great then for them to be able to reject their younger selves. They retain simultaneously the memory of the circumstances imposed upon them and the recollection of how they dealt with the circumstances, thus asserting, also simultaneously, that war is an ignoble massacre to be avoided at all costs and that they proved themselves worthy of esteem. The categoric condemnation of war is accompanied by loyalty to the people they once were. The veteran is not a soldier praising war or warlike qualities, he is a man who refuses to eradicate from his life, as if it had never existed, an experience that was unsought, that was significant to him, and of which he generally has no cause to be ashamed.

Loyalty to one's memory is also respect for other discoveries, simple but fundamental. Veterans love life:

> It is not death which is holy, it is life.[39]

> It is not true that dying is the finest fate. The finest fate is to have a long life, and to be happy.[40]

The love of life is an answer to anguish. It was a normal reaction, on coming out of shelled trenches. A sergeant, relieved after four days in a muddy hole under bombardment:

> Well, the unexpected reaction happened, I lost my strength. I collapsed on to a low wall. I could do no more. The joy of being alive brought me down. Quite quietly I began to weep.[41]

André Ducasse writes of coming out of the trenches:

> The taste for life returned and filled our hearts. Life was indeed that powerful and mysterious force, stronger than all trials.[42]

This was the instinctive reaction of the survivor. Now at last the body could breathe. It was 'a feeling of life rising inside you in front of the corpses of other men. . . . The instinct of life rises forcefully, from the guts'.[43]

'We are still alive!'

But this diagnosis cannot properly reflect the overwhelming warmth of coming back to life. Only the survivors can speak of it:

> We are still alive! Oh, shades of our dead friends, forgive us! We are alive, the iron yoke that strangled us all those days has been released. We want to enjoy the moment, enjoy the pleasure of being alive. . . . Look at us! Look at all these men! Their eyes are shining, their faces are not pale any more . . . they can stand up, they can breathe. They are utterly content.[44]

A few years after the war the love of life was expressed in less lyrical tones; but it remained for the veterans one of their most important discoveries:

> This longing for life was truly our deepest and most enduring feeling . . . a feeling incomprehensible to civilians and soldiers in the rear. The reason for this is that life is a privilege that we enjoy without a second thought until the moment when, at war, we fall under the threat of death, a repeated threat that grows with repetition as our chances appear to be used up and diminished. Life then appears to the soldier as the supreme gift, without

which nothing else counts; in our eyes it took on unknown beauties, infinitely desirable, and we ended by perceiving absolute happiness in man's condition of quite simply being alive and confident of remaining alive, with that same confidence as in the days of peace.[45]

The 'indisputable happiness of being out of it' brought a new and powerful appreciation of elementary pleasures: André Bridoux observed this among his companions:

Their greed for life was intensified at the thought of possible death, perhaps imminent; rejecting the notion, they adopted the habit of enjoying the present moment, of making the most of the simplest meal, or the simplest pleasure, like a gift.[46]

Jean Bernier made the same observation at the sight of his friends eating and drinking placidly on the eve of an attack:

Before the war the pleasures of the body were important to them: now they are everything. They are easily attained, they are calming, and do not disappoint.[47]

Two further comments may be quoted; the first is from Jean Marot:

We knew nothing, then, of the most elementary pleasures, which we thought petty: eating, drinking, sleeping, resting, feeling safe – these were boring matters, almost trivial. It would have been in poor taste to appreciate them too openly.
Why?
Because we had never been hungry, thirsty, and sleepy; because we had never been tired; because we had never been afraid.[48]

The other extract comes from the philosopher Alain, who began a sketch entitled *Qu'as-tu appris à la guerre?* (*What did you learn in the war?*) in the following way:

'Tell me, what did you learn in the war?'
'I learnt first to count more on this living mechanism which I used to think fragile. Thus I no longer take notice of its feeble complaints and protests, as I used to do, for I know from long experience that the fear of being ill is the chief cause of illness'.
'What else did you learn in the war?'
'I learnt to appreciate better the joy of being alive. I eat, I drink, I breathe, I sleep with pleasure. Through this precious good humour I am inclined not to worry much about minor matters'.
'What else did you learn in the war?'
'I learnt to like broad shoes and soft collars because for a long time I wore poor man's clothing. Finally, I have lost that bourgeois habit that I used to

have, of wanting to impress by appearances. It's one less thing to worry about'.[49]

It would however be a mistake to stress solely the physical or material aspects of this love of life. First, this would exclude other pleasures more important to the soldier than eating, drinking or sleeping: letters from home, with their chit-chat which sometimes earned for the soldier who brought the mail the charming nickname of the 'kisses merchant'. Also overlooked would be the cultural and social side of food and drink, as of all physical pleasures. In that inhuman trench life food was sometimes more than simple nourishment, it was invested with cultural values: René Escholier observed this acutely with reference to his regiment of southerners and their parcels. The war also revealed the full difference between 'food' and 'a meal'. For eating to be wholly pleasurable it was not enough that hunger should be satisfied: civilisation must be reasserted in a social act which respected social good manners. This is what happened behind the lines, in rest camps:

> At mid-day or in the evening, groups of three or four took their meals together. It was a luxury to sit at a table again, to eat off plates and drink from glasses. And the menu was not always the same.[50]

Similarly one should remember, in contrast to so many writings that glorified the squalor of the *poilus*, the delight in cleanliness.

> I have never known brighter laughter or more intense delight than on 29 March, in the freshness of the morning, when the sight of a fountain of fresh clean water restored our feeling of being clean.[51]

Essentially, the love of life was focussed on a 'hereafter' of the war:

> Ah, if we are lucky enough to be still alive, how we'll enjoy living.[52]

> If you're lucky enough to come back alive, yes indeed, what a splendid new day that'll be! First of all the smallest things, the most trivial actions, will acquire a value which they never used to have; one only appreciates what one has lost.[53]

> Ah, my friend, if I get home in one piece, I swear I will go for calm, for a quiet and peaceful life, at home.[54]

Undoubtedly the life that they returned to was a surprise for the veterans, but they regretted nothing:

> My happiness is not what I expected. . . .
> Me too, I will soon go home from work. I shall eat my supper while my mother asks me about my day. I know what efforts await me, but this world of mine without surprises is where I desperately want to stay. I rediscover it

with love, and I understand its grandeur.[55]

The experience of war thus gave the soldiers further reasons to cling to a way of living that stressed the simple pleasures of family life or gatherings of friends. A German who spent much time with veterans[56] observed the pleasure that they gained from parties of cards or *boules*, family picnics or fishing parties on Sundays. It was a way of life shaped by long tradition and nourished on the classic humanities: the *aurea mediocritas* and *carpe diem*, Horatian maxims of the 'golden mean' and 'seize the day', promoted in the ethics taught in primary schools. It was the aristocratic ideal of the nobility who thought of work as an aberration – but also of their bourgeois imitators, powerfully attracted by the status of living 'aristocratically' on an independent income, without employment, with the emphasis on leisure, cultivated and elegant or simply friendly and family-orientated. The promises of big business were misleading mirages, and the wish for power leads to disappointment. Better to be happy with what you have got. That is the ideal behind 'to live happily, let us live quietly', or the wisdom of nations, 'My means are modest, but I live within my means'. This was Verlaine's message, in the famous lines learnt by heart at school:

> The modest life of tedious simple labour
> Is a deliberate choice that demands much love.

The soldiers' war legacy was great fatigue, infinite weariness. They were worn out. Their deep ambition was to enjoy their life in peace, as a well-earned reward. Hence their insistence on claiming a war pension: to have fought justified a wish for modest comfort and security, identified with attainable happiness. Why should what was fair for the middle classes not be equally fair for the working classes? Reinforcing the wish for peace and quiet, the attraction of daily pleasures within the routine of life defined by family and friends, the 1914 war consolidated a society of modestly retired people, modest peasants and petits-bourgeois. The war turned France into a society of *rentiers*, of those living off unearned income.

The Brotherhood of Veterans

The reclusive or self-centred elements of such an ideal were balanced, among the veterans, by a powerful movement of brotherhood.

All accounts of the war elaborated the theme of the brotherhood of the trenches. This was the norm. What was remarkable, in contrast, was bad companionship:

The man who did not share out the parcels from his *marraine** with the squad, who jibbed at fatigue duties, who picked up one loaf of bread less from the kitchens so as not to be so heavily laden – he was the one who made a row when he was drunk and disturbed his companions.[57]

Anecdotes of comrades rescued at the risk of one's own life were innumerable, and daily life appeared to have been threaded through with copious incidents of mutual care: sharing parcels or 'grog', wine, water or tobacco, all the consolations of men prone to *le cafard.***

Yet despite the theories maintained by many moralising commentators, such fraternal acts were not the result of hardship, the acts of purified souls. Essentially they were not proof of virtue or high-mindedness, but of the intensity of their feelings and their equality in the face of misfortune and distress. In ordinary life it is very rare to feel a sudden burst of emotion towards someone else. At war there was sometimes overwhelming intense sympathy for a close companion, when he was seen pale with anguish, or whose face itself implores compassion and help. Many of the barriers of modesty built up by a lifetime of training gave way at such times, and men experienced for one or another companion of the moment a powerful and warm feeling of nearness which could indeed be called 'brotherhood'. Overwhelmed themselves by strong feelings such as anguish, the soldiers did not guard against their emotions; this brought them closer together, equals in their wretched circumstances:

> In order to love men it is really necessary to have been aware of a trembling within oneself and within others; this is the origin of mercy, from which comes love for others, not despite their wretchedness but because of it.[58]

This brotherhood was a way of living through an extraordinary experience together. It was not a new element in human nature. It stemmed from the situation more than from the men, and there was therefore no certainty that it would survive beyond the conditions which created it. Alain wrote of 'these wartime friendships, strong, indestructible, and which will, nevertheless, have no future existence'.[59] One of Roger

---

*In order to support the soldiers, and mainly those who had no family, many women became 'war godmothers'. These godmothers were not necessarily young unmarried women. They wrote letters to their godsons and sent them parcels. When the godson was on leave he could be welcomed by his godmother.

**Having *le cafard* is being anxious, depressed, worried. It is a feeling everyone can experience in any situation. Soldiers had *le cafard* mainly when preoccupied by bad news, sick parents, or an unfaithful woman, or by the deep feeling that war was useless and absurd. Though an emotion, *le cafard* is more frequent when one is worn out.

Boutefeu's narrators, the Franche-Comté artist Robert Fernier, recounted thus his re-encounter in 1935 with a railway worker with whom he
had spent several nights and days in a shell hole in front of the lines.
'Alas, after a quarter of an hour we had nothing more to say to each
other'. Yet he ended his account as follows:

> Thinking it over carefully, nothing remains of that long and cruel experi-
> ence except the satisfaction of having met some real men among the ranks
> in the front line, the troops who really suffered; of having depended on true
> friendship and never having to worry about knowing if the man next to you,
> sharing his joys and his miseries, and also his provisions when there were
> any, was a peasant, an intellectual, an office clerk or a pimp by trade. That is
> why, personally, I have never regretted the ordeals that I lived through, but
> with which I absolutely refuse to associate myself on parades which seek to
> justify them.[60]

The actual experience of war also represented more than brotherhood. There was in addition a certain indifference, an insensitivity
acquired through necessity, for if one was not hardened to it, it would
surely have been impossible to bear so much horror. Many eyewitness
accounts make the comment:

> You get used to seeing dead men, to feeling them, and touching them. . ..
> Digging with a pick, you break open a stomach. The fellow finds the car-
> tridge belt, sees the D bullets, and says calmly, 'He's French'.[61]

Dr Voivenel noted the soldiers' increasing callousness. Indifference
to corpses was 'part of the job'.[62] Georges Bonnet, the future Minister
for Foreign Affairs, published three sociological articles under the heading 'The Soldier's Soul', which Norton Cru saw as the most substantial
passages written about the war by a good observer, seen from an imper-
sonal or philosophical point of view.[63] Yet the war was for Bonnet a
school of selfishness or indifference rather than of brotherhood:

> The experience of the past months has notably hardened hearts. By dint
> of living with hardship one becomes accustomed to it. Everyone is sur-
> rounded by manifold deaths. Our brothers, our best friends, have been
> killed. Grief has become so common that it ends by becoming normal.
> Thus, little by little, pity died in our hearts. The griefs of each man were so
> numerous that sometimes there were no more tears to shed for the misfor-
> tunes of others.[64]

Soldiers grew indifferent to everything which did not affect them
directly:

> As I was warning one of my men one day that he was in a dangerous

place where several rockets had just killed a number of his companions shortly before, I heard him reply with perfect tranquillity, 'Oh, as long as they only land on my mates, there's no harm!'[65]

This is far removed from the attentive concern of each man for everyone else which supposedly characterised trench life. Bonnet goes further:

> Campaign life provides us with comrades, companions with whom we can talk with familiarity today, but from whom we will separate without any great regrets tomorrow. They will know nothing of our intimate thoughts; they will know nothing of our feelings; we will present only external appearances to their curiosity. Yet, among them, there may be men of infinite devotion. We will not necessarily present them with the precious gift of our friendship.
>
> No one could be more convinced than we are that solid friendships were established during the war; but that they were established because of the war, we must question. War cannot modify the timeless laws which create true friendships.[66]

So here we have two different interpretations, two readings of the same situation. On one hand, brotherhood, solidarity, *élan*; on the other, companions forced to live together and who fit in with each other, indifference, even selfishness. In fact it would seem that soldiers were no better and no worse than the average man. To believe that the war altered souls was no doubt an illusion. But that it was a widespread illusion is a fact. In the veterans' world, once the war was over, there was an insistence on brotherhood, promoted as a constant element of trench life, whereas callousness and insensitivity were passed over in silence.

This evaluation can be explained psychologically by a variation in the intensity of feelings recalled. Brotherhood is the experience of great surges of sympathy, outpourings of emotion. Soldiers who had hardened themselves against emotion and who had strengthened their defences to retain their balance were sometimes overwhelmed by a particularly violent shock: the eve of an attack, a terrible attempt to relieve another unit, the loss of someone close. They were then more upset because their defences had been breached, and they felt pity, compassion, brotherhood, with extraordinary intensity. Against the greyness of daily camaraderie such grand emotions stand out, and the memory of them is liable to be sharper. Complementary in real life, indifference and brotherhood thus acquire two opposite meanings in recollection.

To accept this interpretation one must be sure that the moments of powerful egotism were not as intensely strong as those of reciprocal fellowship. How can one believe that sometimes the personal will to survive did not outweigh all other feelings? But the veterans are silent on this point, and we must therefore consider an ideological choice. The theme of trench brotherhood would be emphasised because it underlay and illustrated that of the essential union of all Frenchmen. Thus it should be interpreted politically, as an implicit denial of divisions within the group, a denial of conflicts and, finally, nostalgia (naturally right-wing), for great patriotic campaigns.

This interpretation does not strike us as any better than the preceding one. Brotherhood is not a subject solely for ideological evaluation. For the right wing to seek to exploit this theme, as it did, it had to see it as a 'sound' theme: a theme not only in sympathy with its own approach, but effective in touching a sensitive nerve among the veterans and sounding a sympathetic secret chord. The ideological exploitation of brotherhood was only possible if this theme constituted for the veterans a 'shared' location where all came together. Otherwise interpretation through this ideology takes no account of either the widespread nature or the emotional importance of the theme of brotherhood.

The Meaning of an Experience

We should be much less complicated. It is entirely human to retain from an experience that element that is to one's own advantage. Ex-soldiers were neither the first nor the last to cast a modest veil over what was less than flattering, to emphasise what was to their advantage.

There was a bit more to it than that. The spotlight focussed on brotherhood responded to the innermost and vital need to confer meaning on experience: particularly on one that was absurd and inhuman. To accept such an experience and not suffer inwardly in living it, the soldiers had to give it meaning. It is possible to live through banal situations and find them absurd; it suffices, to use a homely expression, to wait until they go away. But this attitude is not available when it is a matter of a life-or-death ordeal. One cannot watch death, and risk one's own life, telling oneself that there is no sense in it: something positive must be allowed to emerge from such an experience – a deliberate decision. This sequence can be seen in action in the notebooks of Tézenas du Montcel, a territorial officer and a lawyer from a respected family with 'correct' attitudes.

8 February 1917. Quite a long conversation with Father Plus. . . . He

does not see the 'advantage' of the war from the religious angle: he does not find souls changed. . . . But I believe in virtue and the fruits of sacrifice. . . . I told him so, I believe it, but above all I want to believe it.[67]

Living means giving meaning to what one lives through. What is surprising, in this context, is the fact that veterans looked to fraternity and not to patriotism for validation of the deepest significance of their experience. Certainly it was for France that they fought in the early days of the war, but no abstract concept survived long in the face of the experience of war: it needed something more concrete, more immediate proof. All accounts agree that from 1915 on the soldiers carried out their task conscientiously and professionally. They held on because they knew that they owed it to themselves and were conscious of solidarity with their close companions. This is as far from the enthusiastic and patriotic military man of legend as from the bad soldier held in check by fear of gendarmes or courts-martial:

> At the beginning of the war every heart was full of enthusiasm. Now (March 1916), everything has cooled down and duty is done without the glossy varnish of the war's early days. Disillusionment, weariness, the diffi-culty of knowing what the end will be, hang heavily over everything. It is a matter of holding on for fifteen minutes longer.[68]

> The soldier of 1916 was not fighting for Alsace, nor to ruin Germany, nor for his country. He was fighting out of integrity, habit and strength. He fought because he could not do otherwise. And then he fought because after the early enthusiasm and the disappointments of the first winter, the second winter brought resignation. What one hoped was going to be something temporary . . . turned into a situation that was stable in its very instability. His dwelling changed from a house into a dugout, his family into his fight-ing companions. Life was shaped by wretchedness, as it had once been shaped by well-being. Feelings were adjusted to the level of daily events, and equilibrium recovered in the midst of imbalance. It was no longer even con-ceivable that circumstances might alter. He no longer thought of going home. He still hoped to do so, he did not count on it.[69]

Thus experienced, these aspects of war left very simple memories: love of life, pride in having stood up to the ordeal, the feeling of not having betrayed one's companions, and of having been able to depend on them. The image of the resigned soldier who carried on the war like a trade is less flattering than home-guard patriots would wish it to appear, less gloomy too than certain pacifists would assert. It is enough that it is true.

Notes to Chapter 1

1. Maurice Genevoix, *La Mort de près*, Paris, Plon, 1972.

2. Genevoix, *La Mort*, pp.18–19.

3. André Pézard, *Nous autres à Vauquois*, Paris, La Renaissance du livre, 1930, p.55 (one of the finest accounts of war).

4. We are very grateful to L. H. Parias for his permission to consult 425 substantial unpublished accounts. These eyewitness descriptions were sent to Roger Boutefeu for his book *Les Camarades*, Paris, Fayard, 1966, following an announcement carried in many provincial newspapers. Quotations here are from the accounts of M. Louis Martin (Les Mars, Creuse) and Brunaud (hotelier in Chénerailles).

5. Francisque Vial, *Territoriaux de France*, Paris, Berger-Levrault, 1918, p.58.

6. Jean Bernier, *La Percée*, Paris, Albin Michel, 1920, p.5.

7. In August 1916. Account sent to Roger Boutefeu.

8. Bernier, *La Percée*, p.76.

9. Genevoix, *La Mort*, p.48.

10. M. Casimir-Ludovic Bernadie, Gorses (Lot), Boutefeu collection.

11. M. Camille Moyniez, 67th infantry regiment, 1st battalion, 3rd company, Boutefeu collection.

12. Bernadie, Boutefeu collection.

13. Gabriel Chevallier, *La Peur*, Paris, Stock, 1930, pp.202–203.

14. André Maillet, *Sous le fouet du destin*, Paris, Libr. Acad. Perrin, 1919, p.89.

15. Bernier, *La Percée*, p.53.

16. M. Charles Gavrois, Boutefeu collection.

17. Jean Marot, *Ceux qui vivent*, Paris, Payot, 1919, p.152.

18. Jean Norton Cru, *Témoins*, Paris, Les Etincelles, 1930, places Genevoix 'at the head, no contest' (p.144).

19. M. L. Menudier, 34b, rue de Dunkerque, Paris Xe, Boutefeu collection.

20. Genevoix, *Jeux de glaces*, Namur, Wesmael-Charlier, 1961, p.49. Note this episode in *Sous Verdun*, Paris, Ed. 'J'ai lu', 1964, p.62.

21. M. Daniel Pechmalbec, Albi, Boutefeu collection.

22. Genevoix, *La Mort*, p.59.

23. Bernier, *La Percée*, p.68.

24. Norton Cru, *Témoins*, p.226.

25. M. Léon Schulze, La Chapelle-Montligeon, Boutefeu collection.

26. Norton Cru, *Témoins*, p.184.

27. Pierre Chaine, *Les Mémoires d'un rat*, 2nd edition, Paris, Niestlé, 1920, p.102.

28. Undated letter preserved in the Bibliothèque nationale in the file of correspondence on *Le Feu*.

29. Chevallier, *La Peur*, p.262.

30. Alain, *Mars ou la guerre jugé*, Paris, Gallimard, 1964 (first published 1921), pp.93–94.

31. This refers to the *Journal des mutilés*, on sale at all newsagents. In 1930 its circulation was 405,000 copies, with 121,204 subscriptions.

32. Alain, *Souvenirs de guerre*, Paris, Hartmann, 1937, p.13.

33. André Bridoux, *Souvenirs du temps des morts*, Paris, Albin Michel, 1930, p.32.

34. Genevoix, *H.O.E.*, Paris, Les Etincelles, 1931.

35. *Congrès UF 1930*, p.202.

36. Jean Guéhenno, *Souvenirs d'un homme de quarante ans*, Paris, Le livre de poche, 1964 (first ed. Grasset, 1934), p.151–52. Son of a shoe-worker, he entered the Ecole normale supérieure, became a teacher, then a general inspector of the Ministry of Education. He wrote many interesting essays and was elected member of the Academie française.

37. M. Dubuis, Ronne, Boutefeu collection.

38. Bridoux, *Souvenirs*, pp.231–33.
39. Henry de Montherlant, *Chant funèbre pour les morts de Verdun*, Paris, Grasset, 1925, p.86.
40. Paul Cazin, *L'Humaniste à la guerre*, Paris, 1920, p.163.
41. M. Paul Ricadat, Saint-Satur (Cher), Boutefeu collection.
42. Paul Ducasse, Boutefeu collection.
43. Louis Huot and Paul Voivenel, *La Psychologie du soldat*, Paris, La Renaissance du livre, 1918, p.140 and p.143.
44. Louis Botti, *Avec les zouaves*, quoted by Norton Cru in *Témoins*, p.95.
45. Norton Cru, *Témoins*, p.181.
46. Bridoux, *Souvenirs*, p.216.
47. Bernier, *La Percée*, p.216
48. Marot, *Ceux*, pp.21–22.
49. Alain, *Mars*, p.122.
50. Henri Nadel, *Sous le pressoir*, Paris, Société mutuelle d'éditions, 1921, p.62.
51. Raymond Jubert, *Verdun*, Paris, Payot, 1918, p.90.
52. Paul Lintier, *Le Tube 1233*, Paris, Plon-Nourrit, 1918, p.189.
53. Max Buteau, *Tenir, Récits de la vie des tranchées*, Paris, Plon, 1918, pp.119–20.
54. André Gervais, *Heureux ceux qui sont morts*, Lyon, Ed.du Fleuve, 1926, p.147.
55. Eugène Dabit, *Petit-Louis*, Paris, Gallimard, 1930, p.248.
56. Paul Distelbarth, *La Personne France*, Paris, Alsatia, 1937. Distelbarth spent much time with ex-soldiers during the 1930s and spoke at many pacifist meetings.
57. Marot, *Ceux*, p.116.
58. Bridoux, *Souvenirs*, p.50.
59. Alain, *Mars*, p.153.
60. M. Robert Fernier, Boutefeu collection.
61. Marot, *Ceux*, pp.234–235.
62. Huot and Voivenel, *La Psychologie*, pp.141.
63. Norton Cru, *Témoins*, p.420.
64. Georges Bonnet, *L'Ame du soldat*, Paris, Payot, 1917, p.46.
65. Bonnet, *L'Ame*, p.127.
66. Bonnet, *L'Ame*, p.43.
67. Tézenas du Montcel, *Dans les tranchées*, Montbrison, Impr. Eleuthère Brassart, 1925.
68. Lieutenant Champeaux, Boutefeu collection.
69. Louis Mairet, *Carnets d'un combattant*, quoted by Norton Cru, *Témoins*, p.192.

2

The Veterans' Movement

A common and rarely challenged assumption holds that the veterans' associations were established to perpetuate the brotherhood of the trenches. In the sense that they aimed to encourage camaraderie among their members, this is accurate, even though they pursued many other aims at the same time. Their origins, however, lay elsewhere.

The veterans' association was not in fact a direct extension of military life. True, there were regimental associations, but they were very much a secondary system, representing at their peak a maximum of 125,000 members. The groups which mattered were geographically based: they brought soldiers together commune by commune. Despite the localised style of recruitment, the vagaries of war usually resulted in a blurring of boundaries: when two soldiers from the same village and the same class joined the same regiment, even the same company, it required a rare conjunction of circumstances for them to meet in the same section and the same squad. No doubt they might talk of the same places and the same battles, but they did not take part in them at the same moment or in the same trench. They did not fight cheek by jowl with one another. Within the framework of a veterans' club they could thus meet war companions of the same generation and the same area, but it was not with these particular individuals that they had shared the most significant and most intense moments of life at the front. The veterans' association was not, therefore, the direct heir to the group that consisted of soldiers under fire.

Origins

Veterans' associations were in fact established for reasons that were far more material than psychological. Two succeeding generations should be distinguished.

Notes to Chapter 2 can be found on page 50.

27

Conditions for the Disabled

The first generation arose during the war, in 1915 and 1916, in response to the pressing problems of the disabled. Before sending men home who were unfit for further service, the army had to reorganise their records; but the relevant legislation dated from 1831 and proved totally inappropriate. Drawn up in times of peace and for a professional army, the lengthy initial registration required by law was delayed even more by the dislocations of war. Disabled men therefore accumulated in hospitals and depots, impatient to return to civilian life but forced to wait for interminably deferred decisions. Secondly, the system for indemnifying the disabled was excessively restrictive. To obtain a pension, positive proof was required that the wound was a war injury: but in the rush and confusion of battle evacuation of the wounded did not always wait for their papers to be put in order, and the evacuation docket or hospital label did not always specify the origin of the wound. Unless the disabled man could find eyewitnesses, the military authorities had the power to refuse to indemnify him with a pension even if it was obvious that he had been wounded by a bullet or shell-blast. The rage of a man who had lost a leg, an arm or a hand, but denied a pension on the grounds that he could not prove that his injury was caused by the enemy, may be imagined. Finally, the sums of money were inadequate, insufficient to provide subsistence for a seriously disabled man who was incapable of working. As the cost of living increased steadily – multiplying two and a half times between the beginning and the end of the war – this shortfall became ever more acute, despite a supplementary pension granted in 1917.

Both administrative and legislative action was needed to remedy these injustices. An admirable Under-Secretary for State in the Health Service, Justin Godard, succeeded in achieving proper lines of discharge and swifter payment, which generally doubled in 1917. At the same time he arranged for soldiers awaiting discharge and crowding the hospitals to no purpose to be sent home on leave. Such measures did not however eliminate simmering discontent within the hospitals and discharge centres, where disabled men spent long idle days waiting for attention, examination, or a session of physiotherapy, their impatience festering at the delays of an administrative system obliged to apply absurd regulations. It was against this background that the earliest associations developed spontaneously.

Military discipline, however, was in force in the hospitals and discharge centres: all propaganda was forbidden. For this reason the first association was established in a hospital run not by the health service but by a private charity for the help of the wounded. Established in 1915, the *Association générale des mutilés de la guerre* (General Association of War-Disabled), or AGMG, acquired as president an important disabled personality who was reassuring to the authorities – General Malleterre, Governor of the Invalides hospital in Paris.

In order for pensions to enable the disabled to live, the law had to be changed. This immense undertaking, begun in May 1915, was not achieved until 31 March 1919. Meanwhile, the disabled had to sustain life in the civilian world, and therefore needed work – but it was extremely difficult for them to find employment. The *Journal des mutilés*, the disabled men's journal launched in 1916, waxed indignant on this point:

> On all sides ardent appeals are addressed to the civilian workforce. . . . How does it happen . . . that many of our companions cannot find work in war factories where, despite their disabilities, they could offer worthy service?
>
> Could it be that the gentlemen war suppliers agree with that managing director of a very large car factory who has made a fortune in munitions production since the war began? Did not this gentleman reply recently to one of our comrades: 'You are disabled, clearly, but that is not our fault [sic]. You must understand that we are obliged to consider above everything else the interests of our company, and that we try not to be cluttered up with disabled men'.
>
> Charming, don't you think?
>
> Although there are factories that employ disabled men, some try to beat down their pay even if they are doing exactly the same work as the other men.[1]

Disabled men's pensions were frequently taken into account when fixing their pay. Elsewhere, discharged men were given pointless tasks to perform, and resented the humiliation of ill-concealed charity.

The inadequacy of pensions and the difficulty of finding work sometimes meant heartbreaking destitution for the disabled, particularly in the major cities. Men could be seen begging in *métro* passageways. The *Journal des mutilés* was full of revealing and distressing anecdotes. There was the pedestrian who was stopped in the street and offered a little rosette by a limbless man leaning on his crutches. He employed an innocent subterfuge to win a couple of *sous* from the indifferent crowds:

> 'Take it', he added very slowly, faced with my less than enthusiastic surprise: 'I make them. . . .'

With care perhaps we could be spared these living reproaches to our self-ishness and ingratitude. The Médaille militaire with double bar deserves better than this wretched trade in little rosettes, an ill-disguised form of begging imposed by destitution.[2]

To material difficulties were added psychological problems. All these rebuffs effectively emphasised a degree of indifference and ingratitude that were very hard to bear for men who had already paid the heavy price of a wound or an amputation. The worst was to be taken for a shirker. Such misunderstandings enraged the disabled men. Innumerable incidents occurred in public places: for example, in a crowded underground train where all seats were taken, a self-confident captain saw a wounded man in uniform entering the train and immediately tapped the shoulder of

> . . . a young man of robust appearance lolling on a seat in front of him, and addressed him in haughty style: 'Come on, young civilian, give up your seat to this wounded man'.
>
> The young civilian lifted his hat and replied calmly: 'Excuse me, Captain, but I have lost a leg'.[3]

Disabled Men's Societies

In such circumstances, the disabled gathered together spontaneously to fight against indifference or disdain. In several towns men who had been discharged called a meeting through an announcement in their local paper. Such initiatives were based on no grand strategy, and the various instigators had no knowledge of each other's efforts. Clubs were founded in this way in St-Etienne and Le Havre in February 1916, in Nancy in April, in Lyon and Nice in September, Annecy in December, Orleans in February 1917, and soon in most towns of the southeast and the Midi. These groups immediately opened permanent centres to inform the disabled of their rights, to advise them on procedure, and to procure aid. They approached public authorities, both to claim actual concessions and to gain moral recognition. Sometimes they stressed their civic and social importance, at other times they expressed the active discontent of their members. Two examples illustrate this ambiguity. First a *préfet* who observed the discontent expressed by the secretary-general of the disabled of the Hautes-Pyrénées, speaking at a meeting where the *préfet* was in the chair:

> He contrasted . . . the generosity of our allies with the parsimonious spirit which appeared to have inspired the French parliament and government. . . . He attempted . . . by revealing certain individual cases, to make his lis-

teners understand the concept that the disabled were victims, and that in order to believe this it sufficed to contrast their destitution with the wealth of the newly rich.

His words met with a response, therefore I had no hesitation in immediately withdrawing the speaker's right to be heard.[4]

On the other hand the disabled in the *département* of Loiret wrote to the Minister of the Interior:

> Clearly we are working together as a group to defend our legitimate rights, won in the service of the Nation and conferred on us by law; but, in our attempts at mutual help, to achieve justice for each one of us, to reestablish our infirm or disabled comrades within the framework of a regular life, to protect them against idleness and to help them earn their living again through work, we are aware that we are labouring now for the restoration of normal national life. We are working for harmony and good social discipline.[5]

From their earliest beginnings the disabled men's associations presented a double image, as aggressive agents for their claims and as committed agents of national unity and civil harmony.

By the end of 1917 they were strong enough and numerous enough to feel the need to join together. Indeed they needed to present a united front to the parliamentary deputies who were beginning to discuss the new law on pensions. The *Journal des mutilés*, which spoke for a Paris association with national responsibilities, the *Union nationale des mutilés et réformés* (the National Union for the Disabled and Discharged), or UNMR, took the initiative and summoned a grand conference, hoping thus to form a federation of provincial groups centred round the UNMR. This congress took place on 11 November 1917 in the Grand Palais in Paris. It appointed a provisional executive committee which took further steps to have war-disabled men's rights to compensation and adequate pension rates included in the law. At the same time it organised a second national conference in Lyon, in February 1918, at which the *Union Fédérale* (the UF) was founded. This was to become the most powerful organisation within the veterans' movement. The AGMG chose not to join in these meetings, which it found too demanding for its own liking, and the UNMR, disappointed at not gathering all the provincial clubs under its wing, retained its independence. Finally a long-standing discharged men's club, founded in 1888, the *Fédération nationale* (FN), which had thus far kept aloof because its president had taken no part in the 1914 war and appeared too submissive to military authorities, attempted at the end of

1918 to start afresh by adopting as its chairman André Maginot, one of the few parliamentary deputies who was popular among the disabled because of his war service and his disability. By the time of the Armistice, therefore, the leading disabled men's associations were in being: the UF brought together most of the provincial groups, while at its side the AGMG, the UNMR and the FN retained some significance. It was at this moment that demobilisation threw thousands of ex-soldiers back into civilian life and generated the second wave of associations.

Demobilised Veterans

Why did the demobilised soldiers not join the disabled ex-soldiers' groups? Primarily because the latter were absorbed in their own problems. The Chamber of Deputies discussed the pensions law on its second reading from December 1918 to February 1919: this was the moment for the UF and the other associations to achieve the improvements they were claiming. Moreover they were not always well disposed towards the ordinary soldiers from the ranks: some, such as the *Fédération Maginot* (FN), refused for a long time to accept them as members. Further, the opening of the disabled veterans' groups to ex-soldiers implied that these associations were expanding into fresh areas of activity.

The demobilised veterans indeed appeared both more aggressive and less persistent than the discharged men. They had come back to civilian life very discontented. Firstly, logistical constraints had meant a long-drawn-out process of demobilisation: they were bored with waiting. From the moment the Armistice was signed there was nothing to be done except lay down their rifles and go home. Every delay was victimisation. Demobilisation was also irritating in its petty meanness. In exchange for lost or damaged civilian clothes of 1914, the army handed over a laughable civilian outfit, the Abrami suit.* Men who refused it received 52 francs. It required heightened awareness of their discontent for the government to establish a demobilisation premium, in March 1919. Back home there was rent and taxes to pay for the whole war

---

*When soldiers enrolled in the army, they left their civilian clothes in the depot. They were expected to wear them again after the war. But the war lasted longer than anticipated, depots moved, civilian clothes were damaged or lost, soldiers became more or less big. Hence civilian clothes were either missing or did not fit in 1919. One of the secretaries of state to the War ministry, Abrami, then decided to provide each demobilized soldier with an entirely new civilian suit. Unfortunately, this good intent resulted in a kind of civilian uniform which the demobilized soldiers would not wear.

period. A tax demand as a welcome home for someone who had paid his dues in blood was reason enough to see red, and there was a swift moratorium on taxes (March 1919). The most serious matter was unemployment, particularly in the cities. Through failure to understand the precise formalities to be accomplished, many returning soldiers did not find their former job waiting for them, although they were entitled to it. Economic adjustments added to employment difficulties: among the demobilised men a semi-revolutionary anger simmered for several months.

This anger, however, was directed against civilians. It was directed at the shirkers and the new rich rather than at the government – an explosive indignation, but without immediate or precise plan. Sometimes it would find temperate expression, as in *Le poilu lozérien*:

> It is an indisputable fact that the war has cost many of us our jobs. There is a second fact which no one can deny: that these men, who went and fought to save the freedom, possessions and jobs of all, have truly earned the right to live by working now that the war is over.
>
> Well, what is happening? On all sides our demobilised companions cry out to us in their indignation, on all sides there are loud protests: the *poilus* are not receiving the goodwill they were promised.[6]

Elsewhere the tone was more vehement, as in this police commissioner's description of a meeting of 900 disabled and demobilised soldiers in Marseille. A speaker addressed the gathering:

> The demobilised soldier comes home from the army with 52 francs in his pocket: you might as well say, with nothing, and wherever he applies he is refused work. He goes on to quote the case of one of his demobilised friends whom he had to take in and provide with a mattress on the floor while the bosses employed Germans whose labour costs them only 5 francs per day. This deprives the ex-soldier, returning after 57 months of hardship, of the pay which would enable him and his family to live.[7]

What could the disabled men's associations offer in response to such indignation, with which they sympathised? Their methodical negotiations with the public authorities could bring results only after several months, while it was immediate action that was needed. The most discontented took their bitterness elsewhere, some to trade unions.

Some disabled veterans' associations – in Nancy, Grenoble and Le Havre, for example – did accept demobilised soldiers as members and thereby expanded greatly in 1919–1920. More often, however, this group turned to separate clubs. Some developed spontaneously, particularly in small towns where there were enough returning soldiers to form a local group even though there were not enough disabled men to establish a club. The most frequent occurrence was the foundation of a branch of the *Union nationale des combattants* (UNC), or National Union.of Veterans

L'Union nationale des combattants (UNC), or
The National Union of Veterans

In contrast to the UF, the UNC was not the result of a spontaneous movement. Rather than a response of soldiers directly affected by the difficulties they were facing day by day, it was a hierarchical undertaking, starting at the top and working out from Paris to the provinces with the intention of protecting ex-soldiers, somewhat as a church club protects city urchins from the dangers of the streets. The promoters of the UNC were men of good works, Christian-Democrats or Social-Catholics. They included the indefatigable Father Brottier, Ernest Pezet and Humbert Isaac, son of Millerand's future minister.

This group enjoyed considerable support. Clemenceau gave 100,000 francs to Father Brottier. The army made soldiers' dwellings available to the UNC and authorised it to put up posters and recruit members even before demobilisation. The military hierarchy was represented at its parades, and moreover its first chairman was a general. The Catholic church supported it, and the Bishop of Evreux even wrote to his priests, advising them to establish clubs for the demobilised of their parishes, which could be part of the UNC, whose address he gave them. The *Semaine sociale** in the *département* of Seine-et-Oise demanded exclusive UNC representation in its region. And the business world proved generous. With the cooperation of the banks the UNC was able to offer ex-soldiers a much-appreciated service: the repayment without commission of the Treasury bonds that they received as a demobilisation premium.

The political orientation revealed by such support became clearly visible at the time of the 1920 general strike. Annie Kriegel has confirmed the involvement of the UNC in coordinating management's response: 100,000 francs at least, and doubtless twice that amount, were paid out to the UNC by the railway companies.** The directors of the UNC

---

*The *Semaine sociale* was a Catholic association of people aware of social issues and interested in public policies though not in actual policy-making. They generally belonged to the middle class, such as law professors or professionals, and were active in charity societies or family associations, or members of private educational institutions. They met one week each year and attended a series of lectures and discussions on social issues. The *Semaine sociale* had branches in some *départements*.

**See Annie Kriegel, *Aux origines du communisme français, 1914–1920*, Paris, Mouton, 1964, pp.437–38.

activated the civic unions, which recruited train drivers to operate the trains, and the secretary-general of the UNC even wrote a memorandum to the ministry of the interior to this effect, for the benefit of chairmen of the departmental groups. Although the UNC did its best to remain officially neutral in its public announcements, it undoubtedly intervened to break the strike.

Sometimes compromising – they provoked resignations – such forms of support presented obvious advantages. They brought funds in to the UNC, which benefited further from a whole network of relationships among the conventional bourgeoisie of the French provinces; almost everywhere the union found Catholics sufficiently receptive and devout to establish branches, and its growth was spectacular. Inaugurated on 11 November 1918, it had 317,000 members by the time of its 1921 conference, overtaking the 250,000-strong UF and all the other clubs.[8]

Such initial successes were not however permanent. The UNC – like the other associations – recruited numerous new members in the urgency of demobilisation and readaptation to civilian life: but not all members renewed their subscriptions. When the lists were brought up to date a heavy loss of numbers was apparent; after this dramatic expansion it was now a matter of endurance.

History of a Mass Movement

The disabled ex-soldiers' association and the UNC did not develop in a precisely parallel manner between 1920 and 1926. The UNC went through a difficult period, and by 1923 its membership had diminished by at least a third. The presence of its secretary-general, Charles Bertrand, among the conservative majority of the *bleu horizon* Chamber of Deputies created a delicate problem after the victory of the 'Cartel', the 1924 left coalition. Supporting open hostility to the new government, he was disowned and had to resign. After the incontrovertible moral authority of Humbert Isaac,* when Henri Rossignol** took on the management of the UNC in 1926, it had still not recovered its 1921 numbers.

---

*An engineer and an entrepreneur in the chemical field, a devoted Catholic activist, Humbert Isaac was living in Lyon, and had insufficient time to chair the UNC for several years. He was one of the sons of the Minister of Trade in the Millerand cabinet in 1920.

**A professional in the field of insurance, Henri Rossignol chaired the UNC until the Stavisky scandal of 1934 in which his name was quoted, though he was not actually involved. He resigned from the chair of the UNC but remained one of its top executives.

After one or two years of consolidation the disabled ex-soldiers' associations in contrast achieved a slow but steady advance. The UF reached a membership of 345,000 in 1926 and, although on a much smaller scale, the other associations expanded at the same pace, a result of their effectiveness in making claims for the particular benefit to their members. On the eve of the 1924 election the major national associations – including the UNC, although its members were less affected – united to present candidates with a single dossier of claims, and demanded from them a written promise to defend it. Heading the list was a review of pensions, to relate them to price increases. Most of the candidates undertook this commitment out of fear of stigmatisation by their constituency veterans' newspaper; but the associations demanded fulfilment of their promises, and by means of a cleverly orchestrated campaign they finally extracted from the government, despite its financial difficulties, an 80% revaluation of pensions.

This campaign, extended in June 1926 by action against the Washington agreements on inter-allied debt, accustomed the associations to working together. Could they go further and create an organic union among themselves? There had already been an attempt in this direction in 1923, but, directed without finesse against the headquarters of the major associations, it had led only to the creation of yet another national federation. This, the *Semaine du combattant*, (The Veteran's Week), established a fairly loose link between the hitherto jealously independent departmental associations.

This awkward precedent encouraged caution. The enterprise was led by two men, Henri Pichot and André Linville. Pichot was educated at a teacher training college and taught in the senior primary school for boys in Orleans. Wounded and taken prisoner in 1914, he was repatriated on health grounds, founded the Disabled Men's Association in the Loiret *département*, and swiftly took a decisive role at the heart of the UF, of which he had been the chairman. A man of boundless commitment, warmly goodnatured and sociable, his integrity and disinterestedness were never in dispute – moreover he turned down a place as a parliamentary *Député*. Apart from this, he was a remarkable public speaker and indefatigable journalist, which is how he met Linville. In contrast with Pichot, Linville was neither a genuine ex-soldier – he never possessed a veteran's card – nor a militant volunteer, but a professional journalist. He succeeded in becoming the director and principal proprietor of the *Journal des mutilés*, where he exercised within the ex-soldiers' world an authority that was simultaneously good-natured and supercilious. Capable of relentless personal attacks, impeccably well-informed, assured of good medical and legal advice, independent of all associations and nonetheless prosperous, the *Journal des mutilés* was a power to be reckoned with at all levels. It was from this pulpit that Pichot launched to all the clubs a major call for a joint conference of associations with full representation for all.

The gathering was organised so successfully, with tact, skill and sufficient caution to avoid any sense of pressure, that a vast joint conference opened at Versailles on 11 November 1927, grandiloquently entitled 'The States General of Ravaged France'.* This led to a national confederation which left each association independent but which coordinated collaboration.

The national confederation had a difficult beginning, and there were fears that it would be paralysed by the rivalry between the UF and the UNC. The two associations differed notably over foreign policy. The UF established regular contacts with German clubs of republican ex-soldiers, at the heart of the C.I.A.M.A.C. (*Conférence internationale des associations de mutilés et d'anciens combattants*, the International Conference of Disabled Men and Veteran's Associations); thus it defended Briand's policies, with which the UNC disagreed. This conflict was settled at the end of 1929, at the end of an outspoken debate. By the crushing majority of 123 votes to 52 the confederation's national council adopted the following statement:

> Faithful to the memory of our noble war dead who gave their lives to end all war,
>
> Convinced that it is impossible to achieve this lofty aim except through the practical and joint international operation of arbitration, security and disarmament,
>
> The Conseil national de la Confédération nationale expresses to M. Aristide Briand the gratitude of the survivors of the Great War for his actions leading toward the realisation of this triple aim, the rapprochement of nations and the definitive achievement of outlawing war.[9]

To get out of the crisis created by the vote on this statement the Confederation appointed a secretary-general who was not a member of

---

*The French words are: "Les Etats-Généraux de la France meurtrie". The Etats-Généraux were under the monarchy the only institution which could pretend to represent the people. Louis XVI convened the Etats-Généraux in May 1789 and this resulted in the French Revolution. When leaders of a social group in France want to launch a solemn address to the politicians on behalf of the citizens they represent, they call "Etats-Généraux" a kind of extraordinary convention, without any legal or political permission. It is only a phrase, but with heavy historical undertones.

either the UF or the UNC, Georges Rivollet. Sales representative for a
hat company, a mail orderly sergeant during the war, Rivollet had been
seriously wounded in the head by a shell explosion. In 1925 he
relaunched the UNMR secretariat, which was disorganised after the
unexpected departure of the preceding secretary general. He was a modest, hardworking, effective and skillful man, and although he lacked the
drive of a true national leader and thus could not match the star per-
formers of the UF and the UNC, the latter underestimated his ability
and scarcely imagined that this appointment would soon make Rivollet
a minister. In any case, Rivollet managed to get the Confederation
working properly and to coordinate the immense campaign of claims
which ended in the vote for the veterans' pension, in March 1930: 500
francs for all holders of the veterans' card at the age of 50 and 1,200
francs from the age of 55.

Balance-sheet of Success

This period was the apogee of the veterans' movement. In 1927 it
entered a phase of rapid expansion based on several concurrent factors:
unity, at least in appearance, within the Confederation, the creation in
June 1927 of the veterans' status and card, available to anyone who had
spent three months in a combatant unit or suffered a war wound, and
finally the prospect of a pension, even though still remote for veterans
of 35 or 40 who were members of the associations in 1927–28. To
these factors may be added the development of attitudes and of political
context. As memories settled, it became easier to describe oneself as a
'veteran', particularly as the connotations were no longer the same after
Locarno and the Briand-Kellogg pact as when Poincaré occupied the
Ruhr.

The associations' growth was spectacular, both through the creation
of new branches and increased membership numbers. Membership of
the UNC at Gray, for example, grew in two months (December
1928–January 1929) from 280 to 1,630. The Calais branch expanded
from 600 in 1927 to 840 in 1928, and 1,732 in 1929, and the Confederation reached a total of nearly three and a half million members
(3,427,000). No doubt there were some veterans who subscribed to several associations simultaneously, but even after the best efforts to eliminate such duplication the total of three million members seems reliable.
It was undoubtedly a mass movement.

To the outsider it is difficult to distinguish between its many con-
stituent groups. First must come the distinction between generalist and
specialised associations, the former open to all veterans and war victims

and the latter to only some of them. Among the general associations, there was superficially a division between those for the disabled and those for veterans, but such distinctions became increasingly blurred until neither type had noticeably more disabled members than the other. At the head of the disabled men's groups the UF had over 900,000 members in 1932. Its strongest *départemental* divisions were the Pas-de-Calais, with 40,000 members, Isère with 32,000, then Meurthe-et-Moselle and the Rhône. Active in most *départements*, it was strongest in the east, the southeast, the Mediterranean and Pyrenean south and the Massif Central. The other disabled men's federations, less welcoming to veterans and with fewer branches at commune level, attained or slightly exceeded the level of 100,000 members each. The AGMG was very strong in the *départements* of Allier, Tarn-et-Garonne, Deux-Sèvres, and the Paris region, the UNMR in the Ardennes, Loir-et-Cher and Dordogne, and the Fédération Maginot in Alsace-Lorraine and the Meuse.

The UNC dominated the veterans' clubs with its 860,000 members (1932 figure). Its power bases were in the Nord, the Ardennes, Picardy, the west from Normandy to the Basque lands with the exception of Charente, Alsace, and the Paris region. Beside it the departmental federations within the *Semaine du combattant* group consisted of no more than a varied assortment of individual cases and lower prestige, with 250,000 members. Lastly, the *Fédération nationale des anciens combattants non pensionnés* (the Federation of Non-pensioned Veterans), founded by Anatole de Monzie in 1929 and later renamed the *Fédération des anciens combattants du front* (the Federation of Front-Line Veterans), appeared something of a superfluous competitor, although it too had about 100,000 members. It was not a member of the Confederation.

The specialised organisations can be defined according to four main criteria: medical, political, military or professional. First came specialists in a particular type of disability: there was the *Fédération nationale des amputés* for those most seriously affected by amputation, and another, *Les Gueules cassées*, concerned with those suffering permanent facial injuries. Each was aimed at a different clientele, although there might be more than one targetting a particular element – for example, two clubs catered for men suffering permanent eye injuries or total blindness, the *Union des aveugles de guerre* and the *Mutilés des yeux*. Their membership ran into thousands, and in a few cases into tens of thousands (the *Mutilés des yeux* approximately 10,000 and the *Amputés* 20,000). Only the federation for men with damaged lungs or tuberculosis, the *Fédération nationale des blessés du poumon et chirurgicaux* (FNBPC), attained 75,000 members.

This particular club raises the question of politically oriented associations: its socialist leanings are undeniable. The *Fédération ouvrière et paysanne*, (the FOP, or Federation of Workers and Peasants) shared the same approach. Set up in the orbit of the CGT (*Confédération générale du travail*, or General Confederation of Labour), which provided premises for its headquarters in 1918–1919, it too reached a membership of 80,000. The final politically significant association was the radically-inspired *Fédération nationale des combattants républicains* (FNCR: National Federation of Republican Veterans). Founded on the eve of the 1924 elections by a notorious freemason who was editor of the *Quotidien* newspaper, it sought to combat the influence of the UNC on its own territory, but never exceeded a membership of 120,000, with the true number probably considerably less than this ceiling. Veterans' societies on the far left and the far right remained relatively weak; they were not members of the Confederation, which considered them too extreme. The *Association républicaine des anciens combattants* (ARAC: The Republican Society of Veterans), founded by the writer Henri Barbusse, close to the Communist Party, represented slightly more than 20,000 ex-soldiers, while the *Ligue des anciens combattants d'Action Française Marius Plateau* had even less influence. As for branches of the *Croix-de-Feu*, a rightist league of the 1930s, in the Seine *département* where they appeared particularly powerful, they represented 1.2 percent of card-holding veterans and 2.1 percent of all veterans who were members of a club – in other words, they were insignificant. Moreover their style of operation, like their aims, placed them outside the veterans' movement and they never belonged to the national confederation.

In fact the genuine associations on the right had a military basis, like the officers' societies, the *Groupe des officiers mutilés* (the Disabled Officers' Association) with 10,000 members, and the 8,000-strong *Société des officiers de complément de France* (The Association of French Army Reserve Officers). The regimental associations were similar; they included a high proportion of officers and non-commissioned officers in their membership. On the other hand the ex-prisoners of war society, the *Fédération nationale des anciens prisonniers de guerre*, with 60,000 members, and the associations for soldiers who had served on the eastern front and for recipients of the Military Medal – the *Poilus d'Orient* and the *Médaillés militaires*, with 35,000 and 100,000 members respectively – appear to have been apolitical. Many veterans belonged to these societies as well as to a branch of the UNC or a federation of the UF.

Professional associations developed where ex-soldiers had suffered a setback in their career. Regulations did not allow for such lengthy legitimate absences, and many civil servants, policemen or railwaymen were forced to band together to avoid being penalised as a result of the war. Organised on the basis of their railway networks, the *Cheminots anciens combattants* (Railwaymen Veterans) numbered about 40,000, and total membership of the three civil servants' societies exceeded 75,000. Apart from these sectors, the only associations worth noting are the *Fédération nationale des commerçants et industriels mobilisés* (National Federation of Mobilised Commercial and Industrial Workers), with 15,000 members, and the *Prêtres anciens combattants* (Ex-soldier Priests). The latter, however, like the DRAC, 10 arose out of a milieu more political than professional.

Political Partnerships

Such were the broad outlines of the ex-soldiers' movement at the beginning of the 1930s. Its peak coincided with a period of relative prosperity and diminishing political conflict; it was to decline with the economic crisis and the rise of the *Front Populaire*. General mobilisation of its membership resulted in resistance to the early deflationary overtures of Edouart Herriot and his financial minister: then came the events of 6 February 1934. On the afternoon of this day, many rightist associations, such as the leagues, the *Croix de feu, Action française*, and others, had called a huge demonstration on the Place de la Concorde, near the Elysée Palace and the Chamber of Deputies, to protest against a political and financial scandal, the Stavisky affair, in which some ministers from the Radical party were involved. The purpose of the demonstration was to oppose the government led by the Radical leader, Daladier, which was put to the deputies on this precise day, and to replace it with a government which the right could support. To make this demonstration as large as possible, the right mobilized all its supporters. Unusually, the rightist majority of the municipal council of Paris set up its own demonstration and took to the streets. The Paris branch of the UNC, of which the leaders were members of this municipal council, joined the demonstration ostentatiously, and paraded with disabled and bemedalled veterans at the head of the procession, walking down the Champs-Elysées to the Place de la Concorde.

Unfortunately, these rather uncoordinated demonstrations ended in a bloody riot. Demonstrators tried to cross the Concorde bridge to the Chamber of Deputies, and violently assaulted the police. Horse guards tried to clear the Place around the bridge. Buses were burnt. There followed a rather confused general strife which lasted several hours in the night. No less than fifteen people were killed.

These events produced a huge emotional outburst in public opinion. On 7 February, Daladier, who had gained the Chamber's support on the preceding night, resigned. He was replaced a few days later by a government including the Radicals and the moderates, which was chaired by the former President of the Republic, Doumergue. But the main political consequence of 6 February was the emergence of the Popular Front. The whole French left perceived the riot as an attempt to impose a fascist régime in France, and it was convinced that democratic freedoms were at stake. Political parties of the left, unions, societies of any kind, had to join together to halt the fascist threat. This was the precise meaning of the Popular Front.

It is difficult to grasp the impact of this particular day on the veterans without entering their own distinctive world. The main theme of debate in 1933 was governmental reform; the veterans felt that the Republic was giving way and that it must be reformed in order to uphold it. The UNC made great efforts in this direction, supported by the *Semaine*, while the UF and the societies of the left became increasingly doubtful. Weary of such resistance, the UNC independently launched a public opinion campaign which opened in October 1933 with a vast meeting in the Salle Wagram in Paris. It resulted in a vague and moralising manifesto, which nonetheless identified clearly the areas where the functioning of the government should be improved. This was the background to the Stavisky affair. It confirmed the veterans' feeling that the régime was exhausted and was destroying itself from the inside; such was the attitude of the UNC demonstrators on the evening of 6 February. Certainly the demonstration was separate from that of the *ligues* and their procession marched away from the Chamber of Deputies, but instead of marching down the Avenue des Champs-Elysées it was able to turn up it, following an accustomed veterans' route. Undoubtedly the directors of the UNC wanted their own demonstration and matters turned out badly, but their cohorts unhesitatingly believed they were acting to help France live 'in honour and rectitude'.

The veterans were not unanimous in their reactions to 6 February. The UF and the Confederation explicitly disassociated themselves from the UNC demonstration; the FNCR and the political associations condemned it. At the very heart of the UNC there were stirrings. Although some *départements* warmly supported the Parisians, others condemned them, while paying their respects to the victims. Their methods seemed questionable: the street is not the right place to defend order, and stepping outside the law is not the best way to promote reform of the state.

Through an apparent paradox, however, the controversial demonstration created unity in the veterans' movement on the theme of state reform. The right had been convinced of this necessity by ministerial instability and scandals; the left was led to the same conclusion by Daladier's resignation, the about-face of the radicals who reneged on undertakings to their electors and rallied to the national union – in short, by the inability of the régime to face up to events. Such side-steppings could not continue. The veterans' movement therefore adopted unanimously the moderates' proposals of reform, including dissolution of the Chamber of Deputies without Senate agreement.

In order to avoid difficulties with the veterans, Doumergue appointed the secretary-general of the Confederation as Minister of Pensions. Rivollet however resisted the financiers' pressures with some success and limited cuts in all pensions to only 3 percent. Further, he succeeded in having this accepted by his supporters, although the latter imposed the proviso that the government must undertake resolute action in several areas. Doumergue, however, proved disappointing, conducting his administration on a day-to-day basis. On 8 July 1934 the Confederation noted that he had not embarked on the necessary reforms. It immediately split into two blocs of equal importance, and, with a majority of only a single vote – after some pressure to achieve a result – it declined to demand Rivollet's departure from the government. The split was irremediable: for or against Doumergue. Confederate solidarity was definitively broken.

Rivollet's determination to continue as minister until June 1935 succeeded in discrediting the Confederation. While the UNC resisted the evolving *Front Populaire*, the veterans' societies on the left and occasionally the UF supported it. Membership shrank noticeably, but within limits. Then came the Blum administration, when the veterans recovered a certain degree of unanimity to recommend unity through the loyal acceptance of the 1936 social laws, condemning all attempts to extend them or to truncate them. The UNC under the presidency of Jean Goy and Pichot's UF then came together in the face of mounting threats, with a concept rather like a moral role which they wished to adopt. After Munich, which they approved, they demanded the establishment of a government of public welfare under Daladier. The more corporatist clubs, however, took their stand on the defence of war victims and did not follow their lead. War and the collapse of France found the veterans' movement in complete disarray.

Social Pressures

The ex-soldiers' movement was undoubtedly a mass movement. But who was affected by it? Across the nation, how significant were the men who had fought in the war and, among their number, of the veterans' societies?[11]

Metropolitan France mobilised slightly less than eight million men (7,893,000). Nearly one and a half million did not survive the war (1,451,340), some killed in battle or dying in military zone hospitals (1,322,100), the remainder in civilian hospitals. Normal rates of mortality reduced the numbers of the 6,441,660 survivors each year, so that by 1930 there were some 5,850,000 still living, and 5,490,000 in 1935. For every hundred adult men (aged 20 or more), there were thus 45 and 42 veterans of the Great War surviving in 1930 and 1935 respectively. In other words, although they did not form a majority in the adult male population, they constituted a considerable section of it.

Of these veterans it is difficult to know how many belonged to societies, for they were not the only members: parents, widows and orphans also made up part of the membership, in a proportion of some 10 per cent of the total. Including the estimates already given, this means that the associations represented between 2,700,000 and 3,100,000 organised veterans, or almost one out of every two survivors.

In the France of the 1930s, then, slightly fewer than one man in two was a veteran, and half the ex-soldiers belonged to a society, with the veterans' movement thus covering nearly a quarter of the electorate. This central fact should be remembered when attempting to assess the movement's impact.

But which veterans joined the associations? Was there a difference between them and those who preferred to remain outside the movement, and if so, what did it consist of? Was it military, geographical, social or political in nature? And, above all, were the societies a form of war victims' trade union?

It is difficult to say. Many men were wounded in the 1914–18 war, but no one knows the precise figure. The total widely advanced is of 2,800,000 wounded, but this probably understates the truth, and a better estimate is probably between 3.2 and 3.4 million. This is an impressive total: nearly one wounded man for every two soldiers mobilised, including those who remained in desk postings. Or again, for every two soldiers who came back from the war, one was wounded and the other unharmed.

Of course not all wounded men were severely injured: some suffered no permanent after-effects. Others were permanently disfigured or disabled. Some men were wounded twice or even three times. In all, France in the 1930s had slightly under 1,100,000 war pensioners, but not all had suffered wounds: tuberculosis or malaria sufferers obtained pensions easily, on the grounds of their illness's presumed origins. Here was a major difference between the 1831 legislation and that of 1919: although formerly proof was required that the infirmity was a result of service in order to obtain a pension, henceforward all disabilities noted at the end of the period of service were presumed attributable to it and created the right to a pension unless the State proved otherwise. It happened that in order to fill the front lines at any cost men who were already ill had been taken on as fit to serve. The army had difficulty in reproaching a man with tuberculosis for having had it before the war: if that were the case, why had he been mobilised? Despite comments, unjustified pensions were in fact very rare, and pensions payable for sickness made up barely a quarter, approximately, of all pensions. There were then in France, in 1930, some 800,000 recipients of pensions for injury, and 300,000 for sickness.

These totals are substantial and their weight in both social and economic terms deserves attention. They were of significance to the veterans' movement too; one survivor in five – 20 percent – was in receipt of a pension. In the societies the proportion was a little higher, at about 30 percent. This means that almost all recipients of a war-pension belonged to a club, although six non-pensioned veterans out of ten remained outside the movement. The ex-soldiers' movement thus formed a type of trade union for war victims.

This characteristic was reinforced at leadership level. The associations were onerous to manage; departmental representatives needed time to manage one or two hundred branches, publish a journal, sit on several committees, conduct a considerable social undertaking. This was easier for someone without any personal professional obligations. Among the severely disabled men whose pension guaranteed them a modest competence the associations found leaders who were available and capable of giving themselves without stint. Sixty per cent of the national and departmental leaders were war-pensioners (against 30 percent of members and 20 percent of survivors). Further, they were men entitled to higher than average pensions: 41 percent suffered 70 percent invalidity or more, a category consisting of 14 percent of all pension recipients.

This corporatist aspect should not, however, be overstated. Although the veterans' movement was a form of trade union – an essential one, moreover, as proved by the fate of wounded men during the war itself – it was also something quite different. After all, more than half its members had no pension at all, and did not seek one. The non-pensioned veterans formed a majority in the associations and their membership could not be explained by material interest. Analysis by age categories is eloquent on this point: the membership rate was not noticeably higher among the veterans of retirement age or approaching it, than among the younger cohorts.

A Social Meeting-place

The veterans' movement was in fact very much more than a union, because in its tens of thousands of rural branches it adopted a traditional social style, uncompartmentalised and multi-purpose. Rates of club membership varied very considerably between towns and villages: between 70 and 80 percent of card-holding veterans belonged to societies in villages or small towns, against 50–60 percent in the cities, and 38.8 percent in Paris. In rural areas, membership of a society if there was one – which was the case in two villages out of three – was taken for granted. The society's national affiliation, unknown to many, was of little importance: the organisation itself was unique and it was essential. It assumed a traditional form of social life, somewhat similar to a lay brotherhood. It maintained the cult of the noble dead – its 'patrons' – but it also looked outward, to other activities. Uniting the majority of adults at a time where there was a particular dearth of young people, as much because of demography – the 'lost generation' of the war – as because of the rural exodus, the association quite naturally played a major part in the organisation of collective fetes, outings and visits. At the same time it was a mutual aid society; and it was, finally, a window on to the outside world – its member· wished to hear the great questions of national life discussed there.

The associations were affected by their social make-up. Industrial workers were under-represented; they were certainly present, and in some number – 33.4 percent in the Aisne, 21.6 percent in Loire-et-Cher, 37.5 percent in the Seine: these were not inconsiderable elements. The fact remains, however, that the societies' centre of gravity tended towards rural society, representing peasants rather more than urban workers.

This difference between membership of the associations and the population as a whole is fundamental. The under-representation of workers and over-representation of the rural world gave the veterans' movement its distinctive character. Other differences also deserve attention. The world of commerce and small traders, in particular, was also more substantially represented in the associations than in the nation as a whole, as were shop employees and clerical staff, while the numbers of the bourgeoisie matched their average representation in society. The veterans' societies cannot therefore be defined solely by their dominant rural element: they were also, for the non-unionised middle classes, a select place for meeting together, for self-expression, and perhaps for action.

So far, however, we have considered the societies as a whole. Was there no variation at all between their membership profiles? Did their political orientations not entail any consequences regarding recruitment? Such was indeed generally the case. It is possible to examine some specific situations in detail.[12] In the *département* of Loire-et-Cher, for example, unskilled workers, day-workers and labourers joined the UNC or its slightly more left-wing rival the UNMR without any distinction between the two. Only workers protected by statute, the most heavily unionised – railwaymen, roadmakers and public service workers – showed reservations about the more right-wing association. The same characteristic was also apparent in the Aisne. Twenty-five percent of skilled workers in the Seine were members of the UNC (the average of card-holders being 24.8 percent) and 10.3 percent of unskilled workers (average: 10.6 percent). This is appreciably fewer than the left-wing societies (ARAC, FOP, FNCR, and similar societies), where the percentages were 33.4 and 13.8 respectively. But the UNC was much more powerful than these societies and overall included more workers. Conversely, it did not appear as a bourgeois organization, having a proportion of senior managers and liberal professions (8.1 percent) scarcely below the average (8.3 percent). The true bourgeois societies were the regimental associations: not only did they include an impressive proportion of officers and non-commissioned officers (23.9 percent of officers and 31.3 percent of n.c.o.s in the Seine, against 7.1 and 18.8 percent in the UNC and, for card-holders overall, 5.6 and 17.6 percent), but the upper socio-professional categories made up 26.1 percent of members in that *département*. However, these societies with a strong social bias were relatively powerless overall: their membership may be estimated at 125,000, within a three million-strong movement. Beside these big battalions of the UF and the UNC the socially and politically oriented societies, on the right or on the left, constituted scarcely more than a squad.

The sociology of the veterans' associations thus relates to their objectives. The big societies stated their apolitical nature and addressed veterans as a whole: they recruited from all social backgrounds, with no distinctions apart from those arising from their markedly rural nature. Conversely societies that were by definition narrower, political, or military, affected only a tiny minority of veterans (approximately 10 percent of those who joined a society), but, in contrast, their recruitment was socially unbalanced. There is nothing surprising in this.

The Structure

Analysis of the recruitment of leaders of veterans' groups appears more fruitful. Branch chairmen were still very close to the members, but the *départemental* and national leaders came from higher social classes, which were moreover not exactly the same for each of the major societies. An analysis of 632 representatives makes it possible to identify some interesting differences in this respect, as seen in the following table:

Table 1. Social Status of Veterans' Leaders

	Overall	UF	UNC
Liberal professions and Senior management (private sector)	25.8%	12.8%	46.4%
Senior management (public sector)	6.2	7.9	3.6
Shopkeepers, small trades	16.4	21.7	16.7
Middle management (private sector)	6.3	3.4	8.0
Middle management (public sector)	15.0	28.6	1.4
Employees (public & private)	13.4	15.3	8.0
Workers, farm workers	3.9	3.9	0
Various and unspecified	12.5	6.4	15.9

The industrial and agricultural workers who everywhere made up the bulk of the membership (60.5 percent in the Aisne, 68.8 percent in Loire-et-Cher) took no part whatever in the societies' leadership structure, the middle classes being preponderant in this role. Owners of small businesses, artisans, middle managers, employees and minor civil servants made up more than the half of the veterans' leaders (51.1 percent), while senior managers and the liberal professions only supplied one third (32 percent); national representatives, on the other hand, generally came from slightly higher social backgrounds than leaders in the *départements.* Despite what might have been expected, the bourgeoisie proper did not hold the majority of posts. At the head of the ex-soldiers' movement there were indeed lawyers such as Edmond Bloch and Henri Lévèque in the AGMG, or Henri Chatenet of the UNMR, insurance brokers such as Henri Rossignol (UNC), or university lecturers such as René Cassin (UF). But there were more teachers from senior primary schools, such as Henri Pichot and Maurice Randoux, tax officials such as Brousmiche (UF), and commercial travellers such as Rivollet.

Nor was it inevitable that the major societies, similar in their clientele, should also be similar in their social structure. The UNC was noticeably more bourgeois than the UF: it allotted half as many places to shop or clerical employees on its staff, but inversely four times as many to members of the liberal professions, and to senior management from the private sector. Above all, its leaders did not come from the same professional and ideological background. The UF was dominated by middle and upper managers from the public sector (36.5 percent); teachers in junior or senior schools or universities and heads of town hall or *préfecture* offices were to the fore, followed by owners of small commercial businesses and middlemen. The UNC, on the other hand, appeared to resist any connection with the public sector (5 percent). Here clearly were different networks of social and ideological solidarity, laden with political implications. Secularity obviously did not have equal value with both, and the split between right and left remained sociologically perceptible.

Differences of structure were accompanied by politically-related forms of organisation and leadership. The UNC gave more space than the UF to tradional leaders of society, but it was the former society that was preeminent in the 'areas of accepted dependency', to borrow Pierre Barral's expression.13 Its meetings were deferential gatherings round chairmen recognised by reason of their personal circumstances as much as for services rendered, and in Anjou it was even possible to see a formal 'chairman's induction' similar to the installation of a military commander, at the head of a regional group. The UF's predominant social forms were more egalitarian, more republican: the concern to respect legal regulations was greater. Elections were by secret ballot, while the UNC usually voted by show of hands – although this did not exclude democratic discussion, as could be seen on important occasions. UF branches and federations sent delegates to their national network: often the chairman or secretary, but they made their own decisions on the matter. In the UNC the hierarchical pattern appeared obvious, and the chairmen represented their groups as of right. There are many other details which would confirm such shades of difference.

Despite such differences of attitude – here more republican, there more conservative – and despite variations in the social status of the staff running the societies, the veterans' movement was a mass movement, predominantly popular and above all rural, under the leadership of the modest bourgeoisie, or of the middle classes. It was not in the hands either of the aristocracy or of the upper bourgeoisie of the business world, or even of the traditional bourgeoisie of lawyers and landowners, even though their participation was by no means negligible. This great assembly of farmworkers, employees and industrial workers was led, in essence, by commercial travellers, office managers, and teachers.

This leads to a problem of interpretation, in the face of the stance asserted by the spokesmen of the veterans' movement. Was it, as they claimed, a generational or a class-based response? Were they reflecting the feelings of soldiers or those of commercial clerks and middlemen? Were they speaking as ex-soldiers or as petit-bourgeois civilians? Both, no doubt – and, based on a delicate equilibrium, variable according to circumstances and problems. We shall endeavour to assess the exact balance.

Notes to Chapter 2

1. *Journal des mutilés*, 1 March 1917.

2. *Journal des mutilés*, 18 August 1917.

3. *Journal des mutilés*, 1 April 1917.

4. Letter from the *préfet* to the Minister of the Interior dated 26 September 1918, Archives nationales, F 7/13243.

5. Official record of the administrative council of the *Mutilés du Loiret*, 1 April 1917.

6. *Le Poilu lozérien*, September 1919.

7. Report of 17 March 1919, Archives nationales, F 7/13243.

8. The AGMG, which was larger than the FN and the UNMR, had 34,700 members at that time.

9. Typed report: *Le Conseil national des 23-24 novembre 1929*, Paris, Confédération nationale des anciens combattants et victimes de la guerre, Impr. Durassié, undated.

10. *La Ligue des Droits du religieux ancien combattant* (The League of the Rights of Veteran Clerics) was founded in 1924 to combat the Cartel's lay policy.

11. The second part of the author's thesis (see note 1, page 2) provides the necessary justification for this argument, in which the figures differ appreciably from those generally accepted.

12. As the material available in the departmental archives scarcely allows us to analyse the sociology of the societies' membership, only a few departments are studied here.

13. See Pierre Barral, *Les Agrariens français, de Méline à Pisani*, Paris, A.Colin (Presses de la Fédération Nationale des Sciences Politiques), 1966.

3

Antimilitarism and Pacifism

To look on veterans' associations as aggressive militarist organisations is to be seriously mistaken. It was a common mistake, particularly on the left. Thus it was that on 11 November 1932 the socialist mayor of Grenoble attempted to ban the veterans from taking part in unveiling the memorial to the dead drawn up in ranks and with their banners, which he referred to as 'military and warlike emblems'. The society refused point blank, and the mayor finally had to concede.[1]

The indignant protests of the veterans in the face of such accusations are not, however, conclusive evidence. We would be less positive if the proof were less overwhelming: the antimilitarism of the veterans was evident, seen not only in their style of organisation and their activities, but in the opinions they expressed, notably on war and peace.

Rejection of Military Organisation

This was one of the characteristics which divided the *Croix-de-Feu* supporters most sharply from the veterans' movement. Colonel de La Rocque had in fact modelled his league on military lines. The 'mess rules', in particular, based on three 'divisions' further subdivided into 'groups' and 'hands' of five men, were more reminiscent of a regiment than a democratic club. The style of command was also entirely military: on 6 February the colonel directed his troops from his command-post, as on exercise.

The external sign of a military organisation, along with a uniform, was the measured pace. *Croix-de-Feu* members had the beginnings of a uniform, and they marched in step. The veterans, on the other hand, resisted this deliberately, to indicate clearly that they were no longer soldiers. In this respect they showed themselves very different from German ex-soldiers, as may be seen in this open letter to a German soldier in the UNC newspaper:

Notes to Chapter 3 can be found on page 77.

Here, you see, my friend Fritz, it would be *impossible* to assemble 160,000 veterans in uniform with all their kit to walk behind the flag. Certainly we often meet together, and when we are supposed to go in rank, as we used to do, from the station to the war memorial, our parades are pretty awful. We are civilians. We have no liking for marching in step![2]

This is not a case of tardy concern at the rise of national-socialism. The tone was not very different in 1924, from another pen:

Patriotic festivals organised on the other side of the Rhine look remarkably like a return to arms. Nothing is missing except weapons.

In uniform once again, Fritz and Dudule, today as yesterday and despite their civilian status, goose-step past in front of the same generals and under the command of the same officers.

Yes, truly, these men are different from us.[3]

A German observer stressed the same difference. Paul Distelbarth spent much time with veterans during the 1930s, and was quick to take the floor at pacifist meetings. For him, the French were excellent fighters but not militarist:

The French are appalled to see that in other countries men pick up their haversacks without being forced to it, and march in step; they see no rhyme or reason in it. The vast majority of veterans, who have of course already proved their value in war, would refuse indignantly.[4]

So no veterans' club parade, even if it was several thousand members strong, adopted the military style of marching in step.

The resistance to militarism dated from the war itself. It was what gave it meaning: the troops fought to bring down militarism in Germany, and if necessary in France. Many eyewitnesses noted its maturity. The staff noted a warlike – but not militaristic [5] – spirit in the reserve units, and Dr Voivenel observed:

The more the soldier of this war wages war, the more he becomes civilian...[6]

In the middle of the war, on 15 June 1917, The *Journal des mutilés* did not hesitate to publish an anecdote under the heading: 'I am antimilitarist'. It related an encounter between two comrades of whom one, a captain, demanded to be sent back to the Front although he had already been wounded four times. He explained:

Barracks, exercises, gossip, restrictions – no thanks! Either the Front, or discharge, there's no middle way . . .

And the conversation ends:

'You'll soon be in command! Once the war is over your future is secure, you'll stay in the army and . . .'

The hero cut me short: 'Ah no! Not that!' he bellowed.

And at the sight of my astonishment he added with a grave smile:
'Not me! *I* am antimilitarist, my good friend'.

The antimilitarist who is a good fighter answers the antimilitarist
hero:

> My hatred of war and of militarism grows all the time.
>
> But, like the others, I have put on my uniform. I have lived through terri-
> ble times: again and again I have seen death close at hand; yet I have done
> what some people call 'their duty'. Without boasting, without vainglorious-
> ness, I can say that I have often shown yesterday's chauvinists – who are
> now discredited – how a devil who was sent down for eleven years in prison
> for antimilitarism knows how to behave. I am no more proud of it for all
> that and I yearn with all my strength for a liberating peace.

These were the words of a revolutionary trade unionist, in a letter to
Léon Jouhaux.[7]

The Fighting Man's Antimilitarism

The paradox of the antimilitarist soldier becomes clear if it is understood that the basic resistance derives from military forms of the exercise of authority. The veterans did not like regular officers. They rarely
gave them responsibilities within their units: out of 632 precisely
defined leaders, only fourteen were serving officers, mostly at the head
of UNC branches. This shows a marked contrast to the post-1870 societies, and underlines how the *Croix-de-Feu* marked itself out as different
when it took as its leader a colonel who was, moreover, not seriously
disabled.

Serving officers were reproached by veterans, primarily for attaching
excessive importance to formal regulations, which they imposed inflexi-
bly and without fundamental justification, disdainful of their subordi-
nates. The demands of military good order were thus perceived as thor-
oughly aggressive. Maurice Genevoix quotes an example from his period of convalescence:

> Three days later, in a square in the town, a captain scolded me severely
> because I had saluted him 'badly', only half-rising from the bench where I
> was daydreaming. I showed him my injured ankle. He offered no word of
> apology or sympathy. 'Like you', he said, 'I've been wounded in the leg. Yet
> I behave correctly when I salute a superior officer'. How wretched! But that
> swine – don't smile, Forcrand: this 'brother in arms' was a real swine – and

this swine, with overblown perspicacity, concluded from the dignity of his képi that I could only be a second zone officer, a reservist, and that with recruits like that the French army had come pretty low and the nation was in real danger.

How much time had he had to forget, this idiot who addressed me? That was surely the case, he was back in his stupid barrack-room prejudices, his military inner circle rubbish.[8]

The future member of the French Academy wrote these lines of lively resentment a full ten years after the war. He spoke for all his comrades. In 1964 the artist Robert Fernier, wounded and with three mentions in dispatches, an officer of the *Légion d'honneur* observed yet again:

Nothing makes one so antimilitarist as spending time with the army.[9]

and he recalled having refused to shake the hand of his former captain at a regimental veterans' dinner.

Sometimes the antimilitarist feeling was more rational. The *Journal des mutilés*, for example, scolded the colonel of a particular regiment for a reminder that all staff must salute all officers:

Make no mistake, Colonel . . . we intended to bring down not only German militarism but all forms of militarism that give birth to war.

. . . What we will never agree to is a rebirth of French militarism. . . . You must understand, Colonel, that you are not alone in having won the war . . . and that without the *poilus* . . . and without those comrades of equal rank to you who had the misfortune to be killed, you would not have been able to adorn your sleeve with five rows of gold braid. Those *poilus* and their real leaders, those reserve officers, sacrificed themselves to defeat militarism, not to let those who were lucky enough to escape the terrible butchery use it as a pedestal from which to oppress the unfortunate men and women put under their orders.[10]

This aggression towards career officers was typical. It was rooted in a very strong feeling of equality. Even in uniform the soldiers' attitudes were those of fellow citizens of the same Republic. It was this same reflex which made one of André Maginot's constituents say, on seeing him mobilised as a second class officer in August 1914: 'The Republic, that's really something, after all!' What was beyond bearing, for a republican, was for officers to exercise arbitrary and humiliating authority. The extent to which military power is absolute, and sometimes treats soldiers as slaves, has not been adequately stressed. On this point Alain evoked some sharp memories:

Children are told the story of serfs who beat the water to silence the frogs. But I, a free man, have held a telephone receiver to the ear of a captain, without letting it touch him, because he thought such contact unclean and because he had cramp in his arm. A captain is nothing very important; but during those war years there was a greater distance between a man in the ranks and a captain than between a slave and his master in former times. I have seen men laying boards inside a chalk-dusty shelter because the commanding officer had got white marks on his elbows; these were men who slept on the ground, without any shelter at all. I note these small things because all those who write about the war are officers who have benefited from slave labour, without even noticing . . . .

I ended up by realising that the men in the ranks thought a great deal about fighting the enemy, and that the officers thought a great deal about fighting the men in the ranks; and, whatever the fortunes of battle might be, we were defeated, the rest of us, in that particular war. 'They own us', said the gunners in their own language, which on that occasion proved strong and appropriate; and when they said that, they were not talking about the enemy.[11]

There were worse things than these scoldings and fatigue duties: military authority is blind and deaf, and it kills uselessly, through orders that lack any connection with reality. This was the discovery of the battles of 1914, and many have never forgiven 'those dashing skirmishers who threw you into the assault, bayonets at the ready, from 1500 metres away'.[12] Then there was the unending trench warfare, and the bloody attacks to gain a few metres of ground. 'Ten thousand dead per hill? Is that what's wanted? . . . The war, at least, is not lost for everyone' complained Maurice Genevoix in *Les Eparges*.[13]

'The worst thing, the terrible thing', he continued, 'is the men's clearsightedness, which was slow to stir, but which was stirred'. And in fact at the time of Verdun, most of the men thought that the staff officers had no concern to spare lives.

We used to say, among ourselves: 'If all the generals and all the French and Germans in authority spent a single night at Verdun, peace would be signed next day, at dawn'.[14]

The man who said this was neither a mutineer nor a revolutionary, but a twenty-year-old stretcher-bearer brought up on nationalistic rightist authors such as Déroulède and Barrès. Political leanings were of little consequence in this case: one cannot forgive distant commanding officers in sheltered conditions who through ignorance, stubbornness, or stupidity risk your life more than is reasonable or legitimate.

The Citizen Greater than Army or Nation

The veterans did not reserve their rancour exclusively for staff majors and officers of military spirit. Faced with the arbitrariness of higher command, they asserted the inalienable rights of the citizen under arms, and took steps to see them respected.

Crimes of the Councils of War

With rare stubbornness, they pursued the rehabilitation of victims of courts martial. There was the well-known series of 'War Council crimes', the men shot at Vingré, the corporals at Souain, etc., innocent men shot 'as an example', the commanding officers having dictated the sentence.* In all such matters the clubs – and the UNC was not the least active among them – made determined efforts to introduce laws permitting redress. In one case they even demanded and obtained the trial of a lieutenant who after giving an order to withdraw had let six of his men be shot, even advising them to plead guilty. The veterans' associations protested when he was acquitted; they protested again when the highest Appeal Court rejected certain of their demands. The radical deputy Henri Chatenet – a lawyer by profession and chairman of the UNMR – wrote an editorial leader on one of these rejections of rehabilitation:

> No one would understand anything if the senior judges of the Supreme Court had not taken the precaution of explaining their sentence to us. They decided on this sentence because in their eyes the four corporals at Souain had knowingly disobeyed, aware of what they were doing, in full possession of their thoughts and deeds, after four days of terrible bombardment, of ten assaults repulsed, of unequivocal displays of inhuman brutality of the same order to advance, obeyed each time, but each time at the cost of the pointless death of many brave men. This unprecedented spectacle, this atmosphere of continual death, of crime with French blood alone paying the price, had no effect on these thinkers, as proved by the Supreme Court with the sovereignty that attaches to its judgements and justified by the long-standing competence and consummate experience of the judges who constitute the Court!
>
> Well, no, gentlemen! Here we shall not respect your judgement. Because:
>
> In issuing this sentence you took into account considerations of a psychological nature that have nothing to do with the law. On matters of law we yield to your absolute authority. But when you pass sentence on facts, you are capable of being mistaken. And when you pass sentence on facts of war,

*For full details on this matter, see Guy Pedroncini, 'Les cours martiales pendant la guerre', *Revue Historique*, (Oct.-Dec. 1974), pp.393–408.

with which you are not acquainted, since you have not taken part in it, we can inform you positively and without faltering that you are incapable of pronouncing sentence without exposing that Justice of which you are the highest expression to every kind of derision.[15]

After the judgements from the highest appeal court there was no further recourse. The veterans did not admit themselves beaten, however, and on the eve of the 1928 elections they achieved the creation of a special court of military justice, consisting of three judges and three veterans proposed by the clubs and designated by the Minister for War. Endowed with exceptional powers, this special court had powers to review all sentences of non-permanent war councils, including those which the ultimate Court of Appeal had refused to disallow. The special court rehabilitated most of the innocent victims of the courts-martial and brought these sad disputes to an end.

Reform of Military Justice

This was still not enough: any repetition of such hasty procedures must be prevented. The veterans therefore undertook to win a review of the military Code of Justice. The basic principle was solemnly asserted by the UF congress in 1922:

> The citizen mobilised in times of peace or of war retains all prerogatives attaching to his status as a citizen. He has the right, under pain of denial of justice, to the guarantees granted by the law to those charged under the common law.[16]

This move by Maginot resulted in the adoption of a new code in 1928. Veterans greeted the vote as a victory. Henri Pichot used it as his headline for an editorial in the journal of the *Mutilés du Loiret*. It is interesting to note the specific grounds for satisfaction:

> The reform's chief characteristic is the institution of a body of qualified military magistrates, selected by competition and equipped with legal knowledge, with their own hierarchy and separate from any influence from military command.
>
> Accused men will benefit from the rules of common law concerning extenuating circumstances, reprieve, conditional freedom, and reinstatement. They will be defended by professional lawyers.
>
> Sentences of public labour or dismissal from the ranks are abolished.
>
> Sentences for military crimes are reduced and the new Code defines the meaning of the terms or expressions 'abandoning one's post', 'presence of the enemy', 'self-inflicted injury', and 'refusal to obey'.
>
> Convicted men may apply for review of sentence but unfortunately the

law allows the Council of Ministers to suspend the right of appeal at critical times; this clause will not, however, be applicable in cases of a death-sentence. In other words, execution can no longer be precipitate, or to set an example.

Courts-martial no longer exist.

Thus, veterans, we have fulfilled our duty to those who were unjustly fated to fall beneath French bullets, victims of a barbarous code and the aberration of a few men.[17]

This effective action to achieve respect for the citizen as soldier was, however, countered with a double limitation. On the one hand it did not question the very existence of an army. The veterans judged it legitimate and necessary, as they admitted, provided that no privilege took it beyond the laws of the republic. Their opposition to the army was therefore not absolute. It was, in addition, relatively discreet. The reinstatement of victims of Councils of War or the reform of the Code of Military Justice only roused opinion on rare occasions and made little stir. Many were ignorant of it, persisting on the contrary with serving soldier participation in veterans' demonstrations. Veterans were seen with banners, military bands, the *Marseillaise*, and units presenting arms, and the veterans' militarism appeared beyond question.

Mourning at the Feast

It is important to look more closely. Two ceremonies deserve attention in this respect: the victory parade and the national commemoration on 11 November.

14 July is traditionally observed with a military parade, which in 1919 was distinguished by two details, both attributable to the veterans. First, the national day of celebration was preceded by a funeral vigil: on the afternoon of 13 July the *Arc de Triomphe* was transformed into a mortuary chapel, with veterans bringing wreaths. Clemenceau himself came to bow his head there in the evening, in front of the empty tomb. Secondly, a thousand seriously disabled men paraded ahead of the troops in small vehicles. The purpose of such innovations was obvious: the veterans would not allow celebrations of victory without recalling that war kills and disables. This same advice was given later by Alain:

> Faced with war ceremonial, go away. If you must remain, think of the dead, count the dead. Think of the men blinded by war, that will stir your blood anew. And for those in mourning, instead of getting drunk and drowning in glory, have the courage to be unhappy.[18]

Certainly the veterans were happy to have won the war and we have spoken of their inner pride. It seemed right to them that the nation should honour them: they had earned public gratitude. But it should be addressed to them as citizens under arms, and not to the army as a body, a blind and terrible Leviathan. These 'antimilitarist warriors' accepted the national day of celebration provided that it was *their* feast day, and that the memory of the dead, like the presence of the disabled, gave it a purely civilian meaning. Linville's editorial in the *Journal des mutilés* on the eve of the victory parade is particularly interesting on this point:

> Glory to you! You have defeated German militarism.
>
> It is brought low. We must, I know, watch what remains. But we must also watch so that the leaning towards military glory which envelops us, towards militarism which has its partisans in France, has indeed fanatic supporters, does not infiltrate the veins of our nation. . . .
>
> Therefore we must immediately suppress anything which might awaken militarism in our nation.
>
> Military parades provide it with nourishment. Down with parades! No more warlike ceremonies. No more of those retreats that stir the imagination. . . .
>
> The Feast of 14 July 1919 consecrates [France's] triumph. Let it be majestic, let it be dazzling, but let it at the same time sound the passing bell of military pomp and all its works.[19]

The same concept inspired the arrangements for 11 November. First we must recall a fact: it was the veterans who had the date of 11 November consecrated as a national commemoration. In 1921 parliament attempted to prevent the practice of extending public holidays into the nearest weekend and shifted the official celebration of the Armistice to Sunday 13 November. There was a general outcry of indignation throughout the associations. The following notice, for example, was put up by the disabled of the Hautes-Pyrénées:

> To All Veterans!
>
> Our festival, the Armistice, definitely falls on 11 November!
>
> Our honour requires us to pay homage to our beloved dead on the exact anniversary of the day that the obscene killing ended!
>
> On *Friday 11 November 1921, you will all meet* at the Memorial to the Dead, Place de Verdun.
>
> A parade will form up and go to the Sède cemetery, bearing the Wreath of Remembrance 'to the victims of the greatest Sacrifice'.
>
> On Sunday 13 November the *Fédération des Anciens Combattants* will *abstain* entirely from parades.
>
> The Federal Headquarters

N.B. Because the parade will assemble on leaving offices and workshops, our Comrades are requested to attend in WORKING CLOTHES.[20]

The veterans won the day and 11 November became a national holiday in 1922. Two appeals published on this occasion defined the meaning of the commemoration. The first was from the disabled of the Hautes-Pyrénées; suppressing a paragraph celebrating the victory and the return of Alsace-Lorraine, it renewed an appeal put forward by the major associations:

COMRADES, DISABLED MEN, VETERANS!

For the first time *we have won the right* to celebrate the anniversary of 11 November 1918 on the right day and at the right hour.

If it is true that that morning of 11 November 1918 *was our only day of happiness*, if it is true that at the moment when the cannon fell silent a dawn of prosperity appeared to rise over the Nation, if it is true that we felt a greater humanity well up within us, let us vow each year to perpetuate this memory and to inspire in younger generations *the burning hope* that stirred us then.

COMRADES, MEMBERS OR NON-MEMBERS!

On that day we must confirm publicly, throughout all France, to those who might be tempted to forget, that *we expect to be noticed* in this nation which we saved, and that the victims of war will remain united in Peace as at the Front.

FRENCH CITIZENS!

You who have known the anguish of days without news, you who have feared for your loved ones, you who weep for those who have not returned, *you will support us*. This commemoration of the 11 November which we wish to make a national celebration is *above all your day*.

CITIZENS OF FRANCE, WIDOWS, PARENTS, VETERANS

At 11 o'clock precisely we will bow our heads in respect in front of the memorial to our dead, we will mark a minute's silence in remembrance of that day which is for ever memorable.[21]

Next, here is the appeal from the *Mutilés du Loiret*, reproduced in full on the front page of the UF's national publication:

Appeal from the Disabled and Veterans of Loiret

Comrades, on the anniversary of Victory, the Men of War have the right to speak.

We ask you to put up on the walls of your towns and cities the proclamation shown below:

For the Joint Committee of the Veterans' Union of Loiret and the Disabled of Loiret,

Henri PICHOT

National Celebration of 11 November
Appeal to the People

———

Citizens!

The Men of the War wish to celebrate 11 November.

The 11 November 1918 marks the end of the most terrible slaughter which has ever afflicted the modern world. For 52 months whole nations faced each other on immense battlefields. *Forty million men fought. Six million were killed. Fifteen million were wounded.* Populous and wealthy regions were ravaged; it will take a quarter of a century to restore them to life.

It is *Germany* who in the eyes of posterity will bear the responsibility for bloodshed and heaped-up ruins. It is *imperialist Germany, pan-Germanist and militarist, who wanted this war*, who declared war and pursued it by the most criminal methods.

Republican and peaceful France fought for justice, for freedom and for the law. *The Men of the War* fought against imperialism, against militarism: THEY MADE WAR ON WAR. *Seven and a half million* Frenchmen risked their lives in battle! ONE MILLION FIVE HUNDRED THOUSAND are dead! *A million* are permanently disabled! *Eight hundred thousand* children have no father! *Seven hundred thousand women* have no husband!

French citizens!

The Men of the War want THEIR VICTORY to consecrate THE ABOLITION OF WAR!

They want *guilty Germany to pay for the war* she unleashed!

They want *victorious France to remain the Nation of Law and the Warrior of Peace.*

They want anarchy among nations to be replaced by the reign of law among nations.

Men of the War, in remembrance of the great struggles which we suffered and in the name of *our dead brothers, we are the peaceful servants of the LEAGUE OF NATIONS.*

CITIZENS!

Join the *Men of the War*, be *Men of the Peace. On 11 November*, the day of *Victory*, the day of our *remembrance*, day of our *mourning*, day of our *hope*, join us, let us resolve together with all our hearts:

Liberty, Justice, Peace among citizens!

Justice for France!

Peace in the World![22]

Beyond its emphasis and grandiloquence, this is a highly significant text: the good republican conscience is visible in the assertion of German imperialism's responsibility. But we look in vain for praise of the army or of French power. The appeal to the League of Nations, like the insistence on mourning and sacrifice, is all the more telling.

61

'A Curse on War!'

The refusal to turn 11 November into an occasion for military parades is also explicit. The UF congress took its stand on this point in categoric style in 1922:

> The national holiday of 11 November will not include any military parade.
>
> Throughout France wreaths will be placed at the foot of war memorials by representatives of the Associations of Veterans and the Disabled, accompanied by representatives of the Government and official bodies.[23]

Similarly, at the end of the article which it devoted to the manner in which the new national holiday should be celebrated, the *Journal des mutilés* specified:

> What matters, finally, is that the holiday on 11 November must be innocent of all military trappings. No weapons, no reviewing, no parade of troops. It is the Peace that we are celebrating, not the war. We wish all the living to be free to concentrate on remembering their first full and wonderful realisation that henceforward they could live for works of peace and civilian life.[24]

So what about the flags, the bugles, the *Marseillaise*? Did not the ceremonial programme for 11 November betray these intentions? Were they not a concession to militarism?

This would be a wholly inaccurate interpretation, if these ceremonies are looked at as an assemblage of interconnected signals. The setting for the parade, as its name indicates, is the memorial to the dead. It is not an altar to the Nation, but a tomb. Although some memorials bear a triumphant *poilu*, most are simple columns without any reference to glory or nationalism. In any case, the monument's role in the ceremony is that of a tomb. This is striking in certain Catholic communities where, after the Mass for the dead, people walk in procession behind their priests from the church to the monument for the Absolution, while the choir sings the *De Profundis* or the *Libera*. Everywhere, the collective decorating of the monument with flowers – often with each school child putting a flower or a little bunch of flowers on it – like the minute's silence, a secular form of prayer, and the call to the dead, taken from the Catholic liturgy for the dead, were part of the tradition of funeral ceremonial. On 11 November, at the monuments, it was not the cult of the victorious Nation that was celebrated, but that of the dead.

It is true that there was rarely any patriotic singing. Here and there the *Marseillaise* was heard; it must be stressed that at that time, and for that generation, it had not been annexed by the right: it was the national hymn, the song of the revolutionaries of 1789 and therefore of the Republic. On the evening of 9 February 1934, at the time of the communist demonstration against fascism, a militant Renault worker, Dallidet, was seen to climb up a lamp-post in the *place de la République* and sing the *Marseillaise*.[25] At the war memorial it was, however, more often a hymn to peace, an appropriate poem, or Victor Hugo's hymn to the dead that was sung by the schoolchildren. This famous text represented the purest republican tradition. When people sang:

> Those who for their Nation died in faith
> Deserve the presence at their tomb of praying crowds.
> Greatest stands their name among the greatest names,
> All glory fades and dies ephemeral beside them,
> And in maternal tones,
> The nation's voice united soothes them to their rest.[26]

they were not honouring nationalism in the face of the foreigner, but the citizen dying for freedom: Victor Hugo composed his hymn in honour of the victims of the 1830 revolution. It is whole-hearted republican good citizenship.

This is confirmed in the meaning of the unfolding ceremonial, presided over not by officials but by veterans who symbolically ranged themselves with their banners beside the war memorial, i.e., on the side of the dead. The officials approached to lay a spray of flowers, or rather a 'wreath': it was they who moved forward and showed their respect to the dead. To demonstrate their association with this homage the banners were respectfully lowered, as a sign of mourning. There was no march past the flags, and no homage to them. Symbols of the community, they expressed its gratitude and respect for its citizens dead in the war. This was no glorification of the triumphant nation, but homage offered by the community to the war-dead. What is noble is not the nation, an abstract entity, but its citizens whose names are carved on the monument in alphabetical order, or in chronological order of their death, or, exceptionally, according to their military rank.

Nothing shows more clearly the true meaning of the cult of the war-dead than the monument to the dead at Saint-Martin-d'Estreaux, in the *département* of the Allier. The front of the monument has a central niche adorned with a weeping figure and surmounted with a bust of Marianne and a funeral stele. On either side, slightly set back, are engraved the names of the dead, with enamelled photographs. An inscription explains the meaning:

The Council decided to use photographs to give future generations an enduring memory of the soldiers of this commune who died for France, so that in the years to come they will do their utmost to prevent any repetition of such a calamity.

The back of the war memorial bears three inscriptions set in triptych. The central panel reads:

Costs of the war: more than twelve million dead! As many more who were not born! Still more disabled, wounded, widows, orphans. Varying forms of destruction for innumerable millions more. Scandalous fortunes built on human misery, innocent men executed, guilty men honoured. A wretched life for the disinherited, a terrible bill to be paid.

Has war created enough hardship and destitution? Has it killed sufficient men? For Mankind finally to have the wisdom and the will to destroy war.

On the left:

Si vis pacem para bellum! – or, if you wish for peace, prepare for war! – a dangerous motto.

Si vis pacem para pacem! – or, if you wish for peace, prepare for peace! should be the motto for the future.

This means that the thinking of nations must be altered for the better, by altering for the better the thinking of individuals through wiser and broader teaching. The people must know how to read and above all understand the value of what they read.

On the right panel:

What if all the efforts and money spent . . . on the war had been spent on Peace . . . ? For social, industrial and economic Progress? The fate of humanity would be very different. Destitution would be largely banished from the World, and the financial charges that will weigh on future generations, instead of being terrible and overwhelming, would on the contrary be the beneficial charges of universal happiness.

Cursed be war and its creators![27]

Through the emphasis on mourning and remembrance of the dead, 11 November took on an overall serious and thoughtful atmosphere far removed from victorious exaltation. There is proof of this in the contrary criticism addressed specifically, from a patriotic point of view, to these civic and funerary liturgies. One of the most interesting texts on 11 November is an article from the secretary for the disabled of the Meuse and chairman of the Meuse federation, a former primary teacher, Sergeant Tapin. He considered 11 November too mournful:

Read the programmes for the celebrations on November 11. . . .

What do you find, four times out of five? Nothing but visits to cemeteries, processions past monuments of remembrance, laying of wreaths on tombs. . . . No, gentlemen, no! The feast day of November 11 is not that!

The holiday of November 11 is a day for gaiety, for national pride, for republican celebration, the anniversary of a great moment when in 1918 France held in her grasp the Boche who begged for mercy! You are turning our November 11 into a feast of the dead. It is not that.

The feast of the dead is the First of November, and November 11 is the feast of the living, of the victors, the feast of energy and the heroism of the children of our blood. . . .

On November 11 I would like to see *La Marseillaise* burst out at every crossroads; I would like to see all our young lads leaping and excited, acclaiming Foch and Pétain; I would like to see our gymnastic, football and rugby clubs in their kit and showing us their biceps; I would like to see our theatres and concert halls crowded with the living, in honour of the *Poilu*. November 11 is the festival of Victory, the festival of our hearts within us and of the Men of our hearts! We should praise our race, Gentlemen, and not offer the scent of chrysanthemums for a whole fortnight. It is dangerous and it is too much.[28]

Paradoxically, this virile address brings out the true character of 11 November: it would have been unnecessary if the veteran parades were truly militaristic. The collective commemorations of the 1914-18 war were indeed established under the headings of mourning and hopes of peace, not under that of the victorious nation.

Hatred of War and Pacifism

What prevented the veterans from veering towards militarism was that they did not dissociate it from the accursed war. This was a general characteristic: no veteran could be found to praise war, even half-heartedly. There is nothing more instructive in this respect than following Sergeant Tapin; he who refused to breathe the scent of chrysanthemums for a fortnight, who praised the teachers whose instruction had prepared for victory, gave them unexpected advice:

And now must they [the primary teachers] prepare their pupils for the war to come, in line with the present chauvinistic movement that sustains the bellicose spirit of former times and makes us look like imperialists in the eyes of foreigners? Does it help our nation to encourage such tendencies, does it not mean encountering the great transforming principle of the human spirit which may be briefly halted but which can never be broken, of which the successive stages constitute progress?

Leconte de Lisle and Barbusse both cursed war but did not assert its future impossibility: hatred of war is the first step in the right direction, it begins to make it less likely; after such an epic, this is the new password for the day, dictated by wisdom, by science and by rationality. Certainly if you visit the devastated regions, if you stop at the many vast war cemeteries, such thoughts enter the mind of the least attentive visitor. But if you are not careful the history of this great epic will also with time become a legend, its idolaters will reappear, numerous and overwhelming.

A crusade must therefore begin throughout the whole world for such a curse to pass down through the generations that this detestation will prevent any future renewal of world conflict. This task falls to the teachers of the young, to schoolmasters and priests. They must emphasise the horror of the end of a day of battle: the dead with their terrible grimacing expressions, their gaping wounds, broken heads, hanging entrails, the wounded with their beseeching hands, their dying cries, the monstrously swollen horses, the foetid stink hovering over the charnel-house, with sinister bats and owls swooping overhead. They must describe the terrible experiences of the *poilu* in the trenches and the mud, in the filth, emphasising the disgusting promiscuity of this underground existence among the rats and the lice. They must describe the atrocious life of the prisoners in concentration camps, forced into 'hard labour', sleeping on a disintegrating bed of sea-wrack, they must depict too the life of the wounded man in hospital, the operating table, the mask, their friend's leg in a basket behind a curtain which no one has remembered to draw across, they must describe the mental distress of the man snatched suddenly from his hearth, trembling for his family whose future is uncertain . . . and everything experienced by the man who is capable of responding and feeling; they must emphasise above all the nobility of the soldier bearing all these horrors, but also his bestiality when, driven by fear, rage, bloodthirsty madness, he commits deeds described as 'dazzling' but in reality deeds of savagery or ambush; they must dwell finally on the sinister work of the Councils of War, courts-martial whose very name brings a shiver. . . . Our children must know all this, must in particular visit the sinister areas of the *zone rouge*. Yes, teach them this, teach them this hatred of war, for it in no way condemns the noble ideas of nation, the defence of one's country, with which Lorraine will always be linked. Who knows if soon it will not spread throughout old Europe?[29]

This wish to disseminate hatred of war was not isolated. It was the basis for insisting on making children take part in the 11 November ceremonies. Here for example is the suggestion of some obscure activists in the Pas-de-Calais:

> The education of the young still remains to be undertaken. This is a task which we have no right to disregard. Through the relevant Ministers we can ensure that lectures are arranged and presented in all France's educational establishments. The teaching staff will not restrain themselves in abhorring this odious, abominable deed, of nations settling their differences by taking

up arms. It will be a further history lesson to demonstrate yet again that imperialism always leads to war and to collapse, and that a nation truly enamoured of freedom should not aim for the mastery of continents any more than of the seas.

These lectures and discussions will be arranged for the 11th so that the day may both honour the dead and be a good day of propaganda, a pressing call for community spirit. From this the truth must be felt, that war is the greatest of crimes and that it is equally criminal not to seek or will its end. To work at destroying war, the day of November 11 is available to us as a precious and salutary weapon. So let us give this anniversary full rein and let us expect the beneficial results of its fullest manifestation. Thus we will serve both the cause of the Nation and that of Humanity.[30]

The UF federation in the Pas-de-Calais was in effect at the forefront of pacifist education for young people. It organised a school competition with this aim, which met with prodigious success: 31 prizes were distributed, 100 certificates, 300 letters of congratulations. At Bapaume 500 schoolchildren wrote essays on peace. In 1927 the disabled of Béthune organised a pilgrimage to the nearby cemetery of Lorette. They took their children with them, and listened in the rain to this speech:

Education for Peace
It is you above all, my dear children, who should be reminded of what these crosses demand. You whose fathers were killed and who lie here perhaps, or in another French cemetery, even in another country. . . .
Remember that we put all our hopes, all our confidence in you, ONLY IN YOU. . . .
Indeed we want this fine edifice of thinking patriotism to remain undamaged.
With the poet we say:
    Beneath the burning sun or on the dark plains,
    Throwing their hearts into the cannon's mouth,
    They died, O Liberty, these men died in your name.
    Blessed be the pure blood that spills in your honour.
But with him too we wish to repeat:
    Oh thirst for murder!
Terrible desperation, the suffocating and heartbreaking odour of dead men, accursed before these 100,000 corpses. And the senseless horror of this blood-letting.
You little children must work hard at school, you will learn from the history of France that the finest times have been those longed-for days when weary nations, worn out by war, worked in peace. . . .
You must be kind to your companions. . . .

You older children must assert your purpose. . . .
You wish for this peace, don't you, and tomorrow you will remember tomorrow the sublime words carved in stone and which you should engrave on your hearts: 'Let the nation be united, let mankind be humane'. This is what the thousands of dead would clamour for if they could rise again.
Honour them by obeying them.
Then they will not have fought in vain but for a better France, for a new-born world with the noble teaching of the Gospels for its motto:
'Thou shalt not kill'[31]

But youth was not the only audience aimed at. It was targeted because it was the harbinger of the future, but the veterans wished to reach the whole of public opinion. They had no right to let anyone think that war was acceptable: because they could speak from experience, it was their duty to tell the truth about war and its horrors.

One incident is highly revealing in this context. In 1926 the chief of police forbade the exhibition of a statuette in the *Salon des Indépendants* entitled, derisively, 'Vive la guerre' – 'Long live war' – and representing a dead soldier's body half-eaten by worms, rats and crows, and bound with barbed wire. Faced with this ban, the *Journal des mutilés* protested and put the statue on permanent display. Amédée Chivot, a normally goodnatured and ironic man who was seriously disabled, devoted an article full of feeling and rage to the incident:

When you hear it said, by someone who has never fought, that 'War is a calamity which we must at all costs prevent from happening again', the rest of us feel that whoever said that could not judge its real meaning. It seems to us that the wish expressed can only be platonic, not something intensely 'felt'.

War for non-combatants means the official communiqué or days without cakes, the closed shop or the field left untilled, it is mourning and weeping, or privation, destitution; but to us it means the terrible struggle, desperate, against the soil, the soil that absorbs, drowns, catches at human beings, in a sticky shifting mud, with thousands and thousands of invisible tentacles: the soil in which you dug out your shelter and your grave with the same blows of your entrenching tool; the soil in which you lived, in which you died, putting an end to unimaginable hardships; the soil, the mud made of our sweat and our tears, of our blood, almost as much as of the rain from heaven. War for us is not the grief of others, the wretchedness of others, it is 'our' grief, 'our' wretchedness, it is the realisation of all atrocities, suffered by us.

We still see visions that other eyes cannot see, that other minds cannot imagine. It suffices for one such vision to seize us for an instant for us to be overwhelmed, for tears to prick our eyelids. The reminder alone of our memories makes us shiver.

If it were possible to materialise these nightmare visions, would it not give people just a little notion of the appalling reality of war? Would it not sow in all minds the germ of a healthy horror which would help to dispel for ever from men's minds the possibility of a fresh unleashing of barbarity? Would it not render humanity a true service to make men see what they dare not look at, bring them face to face with the monstrous reality, force them to think of the consequences of certain irreparable deeds?

What was Dorgelès trying to do in *Les Croix de Bois,* or Barbusse in *Le Feu,* if it was not to show everyone the tragic truth of war? No one thinks of banning the sale of their admirable books.

Now there appears a man who through his talents shows us one of these terrifying images of the war. Immediately people say to him: 'Hide it, it's not pretty!'

'It's not pretty!' That indeed is what we heard from the lips of a lady of mature and respectable years near us, who was looking transfixed at this ravaged face moulded in clay.

Chivot continued, raising the tone:

Not pretty! Well, Madame, do you think it was pretty, being in the war? It is precisely because you appear not to have the least idea about it and because there are quite a lot of you in the same position that such works should be put boldly on display.

Will that impress the crowd, will it disconcert them? All the better. You cannot always be dancing: sometimes you have to think . . .

Such 'propaganda', if one can use the expression for this form of education by seeing, by exercising it simultaneously in all nations, would have a much swifter effect, and much more sure, than lectures by serious gentlemen in front of dusty benches.[32]

And in fact the veterans carried on a propaganda campaign of images against the war: in 1927, for example, the FNBPC presented a diorama of views of the war. In Meurthe-et-Moselle it was not unusual for realistic war films to be shown as a gala presentation on 11 November, even in some of the little villages. To mobilise opinion against war it was in effect necessary first to arouse emotion and to impress. Rationality counted for less than repulsion.

Organising Peace

The veterans' pacifism was not, however, based purely on emotion. Although it was rooted in still-vivid memories, although it was from them that it derived its strength, it was justified by rationality too and acquired the dimensions of a moral obligation.

First, it was forbidden to speak in praise of war. At any hint of such an indication, no matter where it came from, veterans reacted vehemently. Here, for example, are UNC members in the face of a declaration by Mussolini, whom they otherwise supported. The Duce had stated:

> War alone can bring out the full value of human energy by stamping the seal of nobility on those nations which have the courage to face up to it.

The commentator in the official journal of the UNC took up the point sharply:

> It is with such lies that war is provoked. It is with such solemn stupidities that people are deceived, that intellects are mobilised, and that the next butchery is prepared for them.
>
> No. A thousand times No, war is not a school for nobility and energy. . . .
>
> War is a scourge more terrible than leprosy, plague, cholera, cancer, or tuberculosis. War kills more than men, it kills consciences. War inevitably releases the lowest instincts and leaves behind moral ruins even more grievous than material destruction and more tragic than even the greatest slaughter.[33]

The indignation at what an article in the journal of the UNC Paris group – who were responsible for the riots of 6 February – called 'an offering to the gods of disaster'[34] is scarcely surprising. But the resistance to war went much further; it condemned not only praise of war, but also its acceptance as a normal or inevitable consequence of conflict between nations. It is this which damned the '*Si vis pacem para bellum*' approach, for the maxim implied a culpable acceptance of the possibility of war. If you want peace you must organise for it. Innumerable propagandists developed this theme tirelessly throughout the whole of France, from departmental meetings to general assemblies. Among many others there is the proposition of Pichot, in Bourgoin in 1930, at the *départemental* general assembly of the Isère UMAC. He began by evoking the wish for peace among the soldiers of the 'war to end war', and by asserting the duty of veterans:

> We call on you to march for peace; the greatest duty of those who fought is to work against the return of war. It is not enough to put war 'outside the law' with solemn pacts, it would be no more than a fragile barrier against war if after condemning it universally one did not set about abolishing the means of making war. . . .

But Pichot did not state that there would be no more war. On the contrary, forces were operating towards a new war. Therefore there was no question of disarming in isolation:

If you are threatened you must be able to defend yourself, but the problem is not simply one of self-defence in the face of threats.

The problem of peace is to dispel the threat, to act so that there is no threat: and for that you must do something other than in times past.

The old proverb: *'Si vis pacem para bellum'*. . . should be a guarantee of peace in the thinking of governments. But, my friends, for 6,000 years people have prepared for war in order to have peace: no one has ever prepared for peace because one should obtain it by preparing for war, and no one has ever found peace.

The shattering failure of the Latin maxim is sufficient proof that other methods must be sought. . . .

We must never tire of repeating that when you prepare for war, you get war. . . . Preparation for war does not bring peace.

This solution leads in effect to putting down all one has on a bet, as in a duel.

We are condemned to the following dilemma: either we prepare for war and run the risk of the fortunes of arms in any case of conflict, or we seek other means to settle conflicts without any great damage to anyone.

If we prepare for war we cannot say with certainty: 'these armaments will bring us victory'; you go off to war and the wheel of armed fortune turns . . .

The solution is therefore to be sought not in an armaments policy but in international security based on arbitration by tribunal. The reduction of conflict between nations to conflicts between individuals lies behind this argument:

Out of ancient ancestral habit you turn your key in the lock at night before you go to bed; if it is hot you open doors and windows, you are confident of being safe, so you are not afraid of being burgled. This means you have confidence in your neighbours and in the police whose job it is to watch over your safety. What is true for individuals is true for nations. . . .

Peace will be the proof of security. It will not be definitively and finally attained until the authority of a Tribunal empowered to settle disputes between nations is asserted, and until this Tribunal has at is disposition the means of enforcement necessary to assure the execution of its decisions. . . .

As nations consist of citizens, the world consists of nations. These nations are living entities and should be considered as moral personalities, operating in international agreement like individuals in their respective lands.

Peace does not consist of thinking that there will never be differences between nations, economic or otherwise. In our country, do we not have people who are always in competition? Is that why they come to blows? Is it the reasoning of the strongest that settles arguments? There will always be conflicts and differences between nations.

Peace consists in bringing such differences before judges and not in settling them by force of arms.

The settlement of conflict by arms has never been final. The loser only submits because he is forced to; and he is already secretly preparing his vengeance by arms which sooner or later will plunge the world into strife once more, to obtain the repeal of treaties, the restitution of land. . . . War creates war; war is never an end. When you lose the war, you prepare a fresh war of revenge. . . . Ex-soldiers do not want any more war. They have chosen between war and peace, the case is settled. The twentieth century will make peace or war will kill us all.

Almost every one of them has chosen peace, and above all let them proclaim it everywhere, out loud. Their choice rests on an intellectual achievement; war is a crime and equally it is senseless. They do not repudiate it not only because of the unjust and monstrous sufferings which it perpetrates, but also because it is brutality, disorder, the blind confession of intellectual weakness. How to substitute orderly intelligence for violent shocks – that is the problem.[35]

Pichot ends naturally by developing the Geneva formula: Arbitration, Security, Disarmament.

I have quoted this speech at length because I have the full text. Pichot's arguments are in no way original, however. René Cassin, Léon Viala, Marcel Blanchard, Camille Planche, Henri Chatenet and some others, helped occasionally by Paul-Boncour or Henri de Jouvenel, developed the same themes tirelessly in every corner of France from 1924 onwards. It would be a mistake to underestimate this indefatigable propaganda in favour of the League of Nations: expounded in simple terms by devoted activists appealing to the common sense of a public that believed in them, it filled provincial theatres and contributed substantially to rallying public opinion behind Briand's policies.

A Cult Figure: Aristide Briand

This rallying was not without its subtleties. On the right it was slow and cautious. The UNC and its leaders lacked enthusiasm. But a certain Christian-Democrat internationalism inherited from Marc Sangnier pushed it in this direction. Above all, the Right lacked arguments against this rational pacifism. Sentimental 'bleating pacifism', advocating peace at any price, aroused easy refutation. But how to ignore the inadequacies of security through armaments and the common sense that inspired the supporters of the League of Nations? Briand was not much liked by this sector of the veterans' world, but he ended by evading criticism. He received the following obituary tribute, for example, from the chairman of the Puy-de-Dome UNC. After referring to his role as *rap-*

porteur on the Law of Separation in a spirit of union among the French, Dominique Audollent wrote:

> He [Briand] was in agreement with the whole French nation. It may seem surprising to have to repeat a prime truth of this kind. But when you hear people say that there are among us 'people who want it all to begin again', silence is not an adequate response, it must be denounced with matching assertions. . . .
>
> In my opinion it is a mistake to believe that the best way to achieve peace is to prepare for war. . . .
>
> In Briand's tenacious efforts for peace and for arbitration by the League of Nations he had 'neither consented nor counselled nor desired a single sacrifice of military guarantees'. These were the very words of André Tardieu repeating over Briand's coffin the opinion of Maginot on their mutual colleague.

One should note in passing the caution of two politicians of the right, both ex-soldiers. Audollent ended by wishing for Briand's enemies to 'silence their complaints in the face of his labour for peace because he had certainly sacrificed nothing essential'.[36]

The UNC in the Ardennes was more positive. Its chairman saluted the death of Briand in these terms:

> In our grief and emotion we cannot in the name of the 'boars' [the name adopted by the UNC veterans in the Ardennes] and in our own names do more than salute sadly and respectfully the man who was the 'pilgrim of peace', the great Frenchman who embodied France so well, with his great qualities of pride, goodness, justice and honesty, in fact the man who honoured all humanity.[37]

On the left, in the UNMR, the UF, the FNCR and the associations with socialist leanings, the cult of Briand was long-standing, deep, and emotional. No other politician had created round him such agreement among the veterans. Departmental gatherings of the UF or other societies frequently sent Briand telegrams of gratitude and support. The crushing extent of the majority vote by the Confederation's national council in 1929 has been noted. As a shrewd witness, the German Paul Distelbarth observed the massive commitment of the veterans to Briand's policy and personality:

> Briand's activity would have been impossible without them, for they supported him throughout the whole country; moreover, he knew it. That his name may have lost its impact since his death is possible; but for the veterans and for the French people he will remain the man who understood their hopes and their memories, who calmed them and satisfied them with his

unconditional, categorical, unequivocal promise: 'As long as I am here there will be no war'. This meant: 'Don't be afraid, my children, I will make sure that the diplomats and staff officers don't spoil things any more'. The French nation's faith in Briand was truly religious.[38]

Humble eyewitness accounts confirm this cult. The FNCR asked its members to get streets named after Briand. Each year it organised a pilgrimage to Cocherel. Conforming to the oldest of popular pictorial traditions, it disseminated portraits of Briand at 5 francs each:

> All pacifists
> should have in their homes
> in the place of honour
> the portrait of
> President Aristide Briand
> the spokesman of peace [39]

But there were other accounts, still more moving, such as this plaque set up near the war memorial in Houdain, Pas-de-Calais: 'To Aristide Briand, from the grateful ex-soldiers of Houdain' similar to ex-voto offerings in chapels of pilgrimage; or these clumsy verses published in April-May 1936 by *Le Fonctionnaire mutilé* (the disabled civil servants' journal):

> Briand, Spokesman for Peace and Guardian of Geneva.
>> He must live on, and splendidly
>> If such outcry and such unrestrained
>> Anger, insult and hatred erupt
>> Against this name: Briand! Against this fact: his Dream
>> His visionary Dream of Peace, Humanity
>> Which his death has set in Reality!
>> Pilgrim in pain, and splendid, set in stone
>> Immortal in our eyes, upright in his enlightenment,
>> Sad proud soul in full flight
>> Despite the storm, despite death too,
>> Briand endures and lives in thought,
>> In determination and in hope aimed
>> Infinitely higher than the rage, alas!
>> Of those who in every age betray Barrabas. . . .[40]

Four years after Briand's death this uninspired poem in a technical and apolitical journal revealed a faithful and touching remembrance: nothing expresses more eloquently the depth of popularity of the spokesman of peace among the veterans of 1914.

Civic Duties

Yet a question arises. Veterans wanted 'serious and rational' pacifism.[41] They contrasted it with 'bleating pacifism'.[42] They appreciated Briand's rebuttal of an unconditional and purely instinctive pacifism: René Cassin, for example, praised him in the following terms:

> Not for one moment did this man of peace adopt the false pacifism of individual and collective cowardice, kin to despicable chauvinism . . . .[43]

On the eve of the war, however, the veterans abandoned such caution. The UNC and the UF plunged into pacifism at any price which induced their leaders, Goy and Pichot, to accept posts as secretaries of the Franco-German committee, to meet Hitler and to undertake contacts with the Nazi veterans' organisation. On 12 July 1936 an enormous parade at Verdun brought together a mass of veterans from all over France, together with Italians and Germans, to swear to seek peace. In 1938 they were active and determined men of Munich. How can this slide be explained?

It was not a case of sympathy for the Hitler régime but, fundamentally, a moral necessity. Pacifism was more than an instinctive reaction and rationalisation. The veterans were not satisfied with remembrance and the thought that wars achieved nothing. For them it was a moral duty to resist war, including the very concept of war.

The following speech by Jules Romains created a considerable stir. The occasion was the twentieth anniversary of the Haute-Garonne UF, on 30 October 1938. He denounced an

> insidious return to a spirit of despondency: 'What's the point?' he whispers to us. 'When matters get to this point, it is vain to suppose that catastrophe can be averted. It is simply delayed. One draws back in order to advance more effectively'. It was a thoroughly pernicious notion which the directors have less right than anyone else to adopt. No more than that a doctor at the bedside of someone seriously ill can never have the right to say: 'What's the point of saving him? He'll suffer another crisis in six months and that will be the end of him'. What does the doctor know? . . . A war postponed may be a war that will never happen.[44]

For the veterans, in fact, the citizen had no more right to resign himself to the possibility of war than the doctor to that of death, and their deliberate blind pacifism might be compared to certain forms of desperate treatment. Alain laid the foundations of this denial, which saw fatalism as resignation and thus a beginning of accomplishment: what a man first considered inevitable he encouraged by this very belief. If he believes himself drawn to crime, he will kill; if to suicide, he will kill himself; if he believes himself naturally and incurably lazy, he will be lazy, and so on. Even more clearly, if a whole nation believes that war is inevitable, it will genuinely be inevitable.

Hence the precept:

> In the way that one must believe in avoidable madness if one wants to arrest the slide of someone making prophesies about himself, similarly one must believe, with invincible conviction, that war can be avoided if one does not wish to contribute to making it inevitable. This is Faith, the queen of virtues.[45]

It would be sinful to despair of peace and it would be sinful to do nothing. The philosopher's teachings substantially penetrated veteran milieux, particularly those of the UF. The following example comes from an article in the *Poilu dauphinois*, under the title 'If you want peace':

> 'Only the mind can make peace', says Alain; 'but not without intent. Through this ailment of waiting which makes everyone expect well-being from something other than oneself. Not to give in, not to worship evil, not to accept it in spirit, to wish positively for what is not so that it can be. If you say No to war, then No it is!'
>
> This is an immense task which you cannot achieve alone, but whose success depends on your contribution. If you wish for peace, prepare for it and join the growing band of those who daily fight the good fight. If people praise the glory of battle in your presence, recall the horrors of war, the millions of corpses, think of mothers weeping, of the sufferings of thousands of orphans, your brethren, and reply: 'NO, glory lies elsewhere'.[46]

This obstinate refusal to accept war as inevitable is profoundly civic. The Republic is a régime of opinion and the citizen is himself responsible for shaping opinion. He has no need to enquire what his neighbour thinks, he must think for himself. The opinion of the entire nation may depend on a limited number of persistent individual refusals. Saying no for oneself, that is everything when each individual is part of a sovereign body.

The strength of the veterans' pacifism is more understandable. Rooted in powerful emotion – hatred of war – strengthened by reasoning on the impossibility of settling conflicts conclusively through force, the veteran finds his crowning legitimacy in moral and civic duty. This is a republican virtue and simultaneously a belief, and he must be faithful to it, if necessary against all evidence.

It is unnecessary to emphasise that such a pacifist credo, tirelessly developed between the two world wars by convinced propagandists throughout every *département*, had to bear heavy consequences. France, which entered the Second World War backwards, had subscribed to this credo. For the veterans, even before the collapse of June 1940, the very declaration of war was a major defeat. Even more than the ruin of a hope, it was the failure of politics and good citizenship.

Notes to Chapter 3

1. *Le Poilu dauphinois*, UF, Grenoble, December 1932, January 1933.

2. Georges Pineau, *La Voix du combattant* (national weekly paper of the UNC), 10 September 1932.

3. Hubert-Aubert, *La Voix du combattant*, 29 October 1924.

4. Distelbarth, *La Personne France*, p.302.

5. Guy Pedroncini, *Les Mutineries de 1917*, Paris, PUF, 1967, p.150, note 3.

6. Huot and Voivenel, *La Psychologie du soldat*, p.127.

7. Eugène Morel, letter to Léon Jouhaux dated 21 December 1934, quoted in Bernard Georges and Denise Tintant, *Léon Jouhaux*, Paris, PUF, 1962.

8. Maurice Genevoix, *H.O.E.*, pp.60–61.

9. M. Fobert Fernier, quoted above. Boutefeu document.

10. *Journal des mutilés*, 20 December 1919.

11. Alain, *Mars ou la guerre jugée*, pp.135–36.

12. Henri Pichot, *Journal des mutilés*, 28 November 1925.

13. Maurice Genevoix, *Les Eparges*, Paris, Flammarion, 1923 (first edition), p.226.

14. M. Paul Larrieu, Boutefeu document.

15. UNMR, May 1926.

16. *Congrès UF 1922*, pp.309–10. The whole discussion is of interest.

17. *La Guerre et la paix* (UF, Loiret), April 1928.

18. Alain, *Mars ou la guerre jugée*, p.242.

19. *Journal des mutilés*, 12 July 1919.

20. *Le Combattant*, Tarbes, 10 November 1921.

21. *Le Combattant*, Tarbes, 1 November 1922.

22. *La France mutilée*, national weekly journal of the UF, 29 October 1922.

23. *Congrès UF 1922*, p.290 et seq.

24. *Journal des mutilés*, 14 October 1922.

25. Robert Durand, *La Lutte des travailleurs de chez Renault*, Paris, Ed. sociales, 1971.

26. This verse from Hugo's *Chants du crépuscule* is often carved on the back of war memorials:

Ceux qui pieusement sont morts pour la Patrie / Ont droit qu'à leur cercueil la foule vienne et prie. Entre les plus beaux noms, leur nom est le plus beau, / Toute gloire près d'eux passe et tombe, éphémère / Et comme ferait une mère / La voix d'un peuple entier les berce en leur tombeau.

27. We are grateful to M. Agulhon for drawing our attention to this monument, which summarises well the attitude of a generation shaped by the primary teachers of the Republic.

28. *Le Béquillard meusien*, FN, Meuse, November 1926.

29. *Le Béquillard meusien*, FN, Meuse, November 1921.

30. *Le Combattant du Pas-de-Calais*, UF, 15 May 1922.

31. *Le Combattant du Pas-de-Calais*, UF, 10 October 1927.

32. *Journal des mutilés*, 27 March 1926.

33. *La Voix du combattant*, 13 August 1932.

34. *L'UNC de Paris*, November 1932.

35. Supplement to *Le Poilu dauphinois*, January 1931.

36. *Le Poilu de Centre*, UNC, Puy-de-Dome, March 1932.

37. *Le Combattant sanglier*, UNC, Ardennes, March 1932.

38. Distelbarth, *La Personne France*, p.355.

39. *Le Poilu républicain*, December 1933, February 1934, March 1934, etc.

40. *Le Fonctionnaire mutilé*, April-May 1936.

41. *Le Mutilé*, journal of the FOP, January 1928.

42. *La Voix du combattant*, 13 October 1928.

43. *Les Cahiers de l'UF*, 20 June 1937.

44. *Les Cahiers de l'UF*, 10 November 1938.

45. Alain, *Mars*, pp.161, 253.

46. *Le Poilu dauphinois*, September 1932. The extract from Alain quoted in this article was taken from *Mars ou la guerre jugée*, paragraph CXI, 'Vouloir', p.248.

4

Veterans' Patriotism

The veterans' determined pacifism and adherence to the Geneva ideals of a supranational organisation capable of enforcing its decisions did not inhibit their profound patriotism – but the nature of this patriotism should be made clear. What is, in fact, a pacifist patriotism, or, to borrow the title of a lecture of Henri Chatenet, 'patriotic pacifism'?[1] How can it be explained that a local UNC chairman could call a departmental congress report 'Patriotism and Pacifism, Two Ideas that go together'?[2] And what did Jacques Delahoche mean when in 1937 he asserted: 'Our pacifism has patriotic origins'?[3]

It must first be emphasised that never, even on the extreme left, even among the few veterans who demonstrated their protest at the Père Lachaise cemetery on 14 July 1919, did pacifism exclude patriotism. It might go as far as opposing the standing army, as far as total disarmament: it did not bring with it any radical denunciation of the concept of 'the nation'. Two examples may be quoted.

First, Henri Barbusse, founder of ARAC, in an article dated June 1917:

> Love France as you love your mother. Wish her great, noble, rich, radiant. But do not place her above justice and morality. You have no more right to cry out to the world: 'France first!' than you have to proclaim: 'Me first!' or 'My family first!' Remember: all men are equal, all nations are equal. It may be that at a given moment the interests of a powerful nation may appear to operate against justice; but even so one has no interest in breaking the primordial commandment; any advantage gained by such means is as ephemeral as the financial prosperity of a Bonnot*. This love that you have for your country with all its wealth of sweetness, beauty, greatness will be better served, and more effectively – because more durably – by making her the champion of right and justice, and of the admirable equality of mankind. Justice first.[4]

Notes to Chapter 4 can be found on page 94.

*The 'Bonnot gang', the 'Bande à Bonnot', was a famous group of thieves and crooks whose misdeeds were largely echoed by the newspapers before the First World War. Songs and films have been devoted to this gang, which is still well-known.

Since the author of *Le Feu* (Under Fire) passed at the time for the champion of pacifism, the journal that published this text was closely watched by the censor, and was finally banned when Clemenceau came to power. Yet Barbusse's themes were not unusual among the socialist minority. They could be found above the name of a younger man who showed promise of becoming one of the leaders of the extreme left, Raymond Lefebvre, under the heading of 'ARAC and Patriotism'.

The origin of this article was a polemic against a journalist who reproached Lefebvre with having spoken of 'military-blue rags' and of the 'misfortune' of being an ex-soldier. The reply is interesting in what it omits as much as for what it includes:

> I believe, in my heart and conscience, that I am truly a good Frenchman!
> To love France seems to me as straightforward as to love my mother!
> And so . . . reading the great classics is the great joy of my life. . . . I don't know. . . . But one blushes to utter pompous words about such a deep and essential feeling as love of France. It's not among us that people should wax lyrical on the subject. . . .
> But I believe that France can exist in the world without an army. And that one serves one's country by serving the cause of full and universal disarmament.
> Antipatriotism, sabotage of mobilisation, all that is the sort of operetta bathos that links the dying moon to the graveyard of its Victory.
> Yet hatred of military glory, of war, of the army, of national rivalry, of national pride – that is a hatred hallowed in my reasoning.
> And it is very important that ex-soldiers express clearly their disgust with the old bloodthirsty Code of Honour. We have no right to take pride in our title of Ex-Soldiers.
> Our great sufferings give us great rights, and that's all there is to say.[5]

Thus on the extreme left the war seems to have discredited 'operatic bathos'. Still more certainly, it discredited a certain style of patriotism.

An Outdated Form of Patriotism

The veterans first denounced 'bad' patriotism. Various defining adjectives reappear persistently: the patriotism that they disown is 'narrow', 'aggressive', 'chauvinist', 'jingoistic'. In short, 'nationalist'.

Denunciation of this type of patriotism was widespread. It can even be found on the lips of the UNC leader on 6 February 1934, Georges Lebecq, from the extreme right, who demanded that the veterans should operate on a 'national' plan but who felt constrained – either through conviction or hypocrisy – to back off promptly from nationalism:

There is . . . a type of nationalism against which one can never react too strongly. We have all known Frenchmen – and it would not be difficult to find more of them – who, convinced of the superiority of our country as of a religious dogma, see every foreigner as an enemy, suspect all initiatives from outside our frontiers, condemn a priori any attempt at international agreement, and strongly recommend splendid isolation for France. Dazzling military exercises, weapons glittering in the sun, troops marching past to the sound of brass, all this stirs them to turbulent heroism.[6]

What discredited this chauvinistic patriotism, even for such as Lebecq, was that it led to war. It was a form of patriotism that properly belonged to the home guard element, to the cover pictures of *L'Illustration* and to discussion in corner cafés, bars or salons, a form that did not survive the test of fire. A minor incident in the memoirs of a soldier in the ranks proves the point, although not written until 1964. It happened in 1916, on the eve of an attack:

> We had a young officer-cadet, for whom it was the baptism of fire. He began on a little patriotic homily. An old sweat who had been through the Battle of the Marne interrupted him: 'That'll do, young fellow, shut your mouth and take command.'[7]

It is impossible to overstate the veterans' hatred for the patriotism of the home front. They detested the middle-aged men who demanded offensives and paid for them light-heartedly with the lives of others – their own lives – like the character Théodulfe, sketched by Alain in the style of La Bruyère:

> Indomitable, in his armchair. Running for the newspaper as to a theatre. Envying those heroic deaths, and rehearsing them inwardly, as a tonic; delivered from sad words by these pictured dangers. More confident against this form of death no longer related to age. Taken out of himself with admiration. Loving better even that nephew of his who was in the war because he no longer envied him his insolent youthfulness; finding sweetness in weeping for him, and pride at not dying of it. Ennobled, uplifted, released.[8]

This response was not the sole preserve of the radical philosopher; it can be found everywhere in the veterans' world; as seen in this final example taken from the report on the Ardennes UNC conference on peace in 1930. The author was not an unconditional pacifist. He wanted to see the culture of pacifism adopted in parallel in all nations, and he places the safety of France in the prime position. And yet there are memories which he cannot forget:

> My dear friends,
> I have insisted on addressing the following important question: Ex-soldiers and the Peace.

Who indeed should be entitled to speak on this subject, if not ex-soldiers? Yet we are hardly allowed the right to discuss it, for among those who are not part of us, for those who lack the veterans' approach, the ex-soldiers groups, as warlike organisations, are not qualified to talk about pece. My friends, this is all wrong.

Warmongers, revisionists, sabre-rattlers, that's all we are for most people who are blinded by politics (using the word politics in its pejorative sense), for those who have forgotten nothing of mistaken pre-war ways and who have learnt nothing from the war.

And those same people, without even trying to find out what we represent, treat us as revisionists.

Next the writer reveals his ideas. Then, having mentioned the demands of security, he goes into a sort of digression:

Note well, my dear friends, that in our regions which have suffered so much it is easy to strike at the enemy in peace time, to insult the Boches or the Italians when there are no more bullets flying around and no more shells exploding. It's all the easier because we all have 'piercing' memories of blows received.

Should we copy the man in the Ardennes, that super-patriot who between 1870 and 1914 regularly tipped several German weapons on to the foot of the monument in Bazeilles on September 1 every year?

He was very keen for us to go to war, but he stayed at home, which means that, now that the war is over, he can write the history of those who were not there.

The conclusion of the report, briefly, is as follows:

So, let us be pacifists. Let us encourage any move in favour of peace. But do not let us allow ourselves to be pushed.[9]

This comes down to the same thing as saying: 'Let us be patriotic but let us never give in to nationalist chauvinism'.

From this point of view the war definitively discredited old-style patriotism: that of the anti-Dreyfusards. For those who took part in the war it settled unequivocally the debate which had divided France since the beginning of the century. Not only did the mobilised citizens announce that there was no right to convict a soldier in a trial that was manifestly irregular (after the reform of 1928 it was no longer possible to base a conviction on a document not disclosed to the defence) but they rose up against the patriotic discourse conducted at that time by defenders of the army: this discourse led to war. It was impossible to forget it, when one had risked being killed in the name of that particular patriotism. A slashing revisionism challenged the chauvinistic patrio-

tism of a cheerful enthusiastic war, as expressed on the eve of 1914 by
the Agathon enquiry into youth, and of which Déroulède had been the
advocate and Barrès the herald. In 1964 a Cherbourg dentist wrote as
he passed through Paris:

> Last November, as I went across the Square du Roule, I stopped in front
> of Déroulède's statue, 'The bugler is old and bold, and when the struggle is
> grave . . .' etc., and I swore at him as I would have done in front of Barrès'
> statue (the blue line of the Vosges).
>
> Each time I pass Clemenceau's statue I salute it, because he knew that war
> was no fun, for either side.
>
> As for hereditary hatred, excuse me while I laugh.[10]

A page has definitely been turned. War killed the naive trumpeting
patriotism of Déroulède's League of Patriots. No one now is ignorant
of the fact that it was deceitful and murderous, and therefore criminal.

Enlightened Patriotism

In contrast to the 'narrow, shabby, shrinking' patriotism of the chauvinists, the nationalists and the super-patriots, the veterans set up a
good patriotism, 'enlightened' and 'developed', which combined love of
France with love of 'humanity'.

The following example deserves particular attention because it does
not come from one of the great leaders of the ex-soldiers' world but
from a militant in the *département* of the Haute-Vienne, writing under
the pseudonym of 'An old townsman'. It was in a long article entitled
'Patriotism', from which I quote long extracts.

> Love of one's Country is the first love
> And the final love after the love of God
> to quote Verlaine's exquisite lines. Like religion, the nation has its form
> of worship, its temples, its pontiffs and its martyrs. The early Christians
> died for their God; we make do now with dying for our country. More than
> 1,600,000 French corpses and an equally large number of survivors bear
> witness to this love. Did the glory of France require the spilling of so much
> blood? Does the Nation, like the Moloch of ancient times, periodically
> demand a hecatomb of victims? We do not believe this, we ex-soldiers
> whose feelings can hardly be guessed at, we do not think that the nation
> seeks the death of her children, we feel that France is in no respect the
> bloodthirsty idol worshipped by certain fanatics.
>
> Since some people have learned nothing from the war, we think that in
> the aftermath of the slaughter the *poilus* have a duty to specify what they
> understand by patriotism. . . .

The Nation is a historic reality which we can scarcely deny. Nature imposes it on us in the same way as it imposes our parents on us. It is a sort of fate to which we submit without being able to escape it. It is a fact, a physical heredity, a moral solidarity, 'a spiritual principle'. What creates the Nation, according to Renan, is the common possession of a rich legacy of remembrance, it is positive consent, the desire to live together, the wish to carry on justifying the heritage which has come down to us undivided.

Such a definition satisfies everyone. Why does patriotism have to take on so many different aspects? Why must it be transformed into a sort of narrow superstition, a dark fetish? To the super-patriots everything that is national is sacred, even the soil, even assassination. 'Chauvinists lay claim to the sweetness of the family cradle to give an impetus to war. Nationalism was created out of the love of one's homeland.' said Barbusse. It denatures and disfigures the legitimate love of one's country. This feeling, thus restricted, has unexpected consequences, for it engenders defiance, hostility and hatred towards other nations. . . . For half a century the 'tricolour brayings' of such as Déroulède, Brunetière, Lemaître, Barrès, etc., have aroused and impassioned crowds, stirred ancient instincts, sustained the notion of revenge, and given birth to the destructive hatred which brought us to war.

Doubtless nationalists do not allow themselves to preach hatred of foreigners; they forget that their negative and overweening patriotism is, in respect of other nations, a perpetual denigration, a moral offence, a stupid challenge. These are nothing but blusterings, irritations, threats, criticisms, arrogant declarations. Such an attitude produces stupid rufflings of self-esteem, inimical relationships, in fact hostility and its dangerous consequences.

This kind of narrow patriotism has shown what it can achieve. It could be said that the last war was its product. That is why we want none of it.

After this denunciation containing all the themes already analysed, the article continues, presenting the contrast of 'good' patriotism:

We think we love our country as much as anyone by seeking to deserve the esteem of other nations.

I love in my country a heart which extends beyond it
And the more I am French, the more I feel part of humanity.

We consider that patriotism is not irreconcilable with internationalism, and that we must prepare for the blessed moment when all the nations of free men will gather together freely in peaceful and brotherly federation. This extended patriotism, in contrast to the other, restricted, concept, does not imply any diminution of national feeling. Barrès, so fiercely French, never forgot that he was from Lorraine. Humanity grouped itself together in families, then in tribes, then in cities, it has always united to make up provinces which united in their turn to create a single State. Why restrict this development at this point? Why not envisage a society of nations? . . .

The writer next refuses to fall into the opposite extreme:

> This literary cosmopolitanism is no doubt the final stage of transformation of the concept of nationhood into the concept of well-being. We believe it to be as exaggerated as the extreme patriotism of our chauvinists. Our love of humanity does not make us abdicate from our love of our country. Glory is not dying but living for one's country. . . .
>
> That is why we insist that people must not commit the crime of teaching our children a type of patriotism that is narrow, exclusive, aggressive. Such patriotism, learned in childhood, becomes ineradicable and poisons the brain for ever. . . .
>
> We love our country and humanity and we repeat Lamartine's lines (*La Marseillaise de la paix*):
>
> Nation, a grandiose name for Barbarian-land;
> Ignorance and error alone have nationality;
>   Brotherhood has none
> My country lies wherever France is radiant,
> And where her genius bursts on dazzled eyes.
> Each man comes from the land of his own intelligence.
> Each thinking man is fellow citizen with me,
> Truth is my country.[11]

This very dense text expounds most of the themes that constitute veterans' patriotism. Here can be found the notion of a continuous movement through which humanity progresses from family to tribe, then to city, province, and on to the state and the society of nations. This is the dynamic theme of *purified* patriotism. It appears in many guises. Certainly it was not very common among the national directors of the UNC, whose concept of patriotism was more restricted. Their discourse on the national interest did not always include any counterbalancing discourse on the cooperation of peoples. Or, like Paul Galland, they evoked the 'veterans who offered everything to their Country and who wished to continue serving the Country in great love, without hatred for the Country of others',[12] thus presenting only in a negative light (without hatred for the Country of others) a movement presented elsewhere in a positive and generous light, in which patriotism purifies and strengthens itself.

In the provinces, however, the UNC was not always so restrictive. In the Ardennes, for example, it put forward arguments which would not have been rejected by the UF. Two examples may be offered; the first is from the chairman of the Sedan UNC who to an audience of 700 veterans depicted

> nations as perfectible as individuals, and the patriotism which for long

asserted itself only through war now purifying and educating itself, becoming tolerant, the friend of agreement, justice, the friend of peace.

And in conclusion, and requesting the veterans not to let themselves be divided:

> Friends, you will not permit such sacrilege, for you want to preserve your country's strength so that it will have the power to bear on high, and for ever, the torch to guide the world towards a better humanity, full of love and brotherhood.[13]

Six months later, at the conference of the Rethel branch at Novion-Porcien, the delegate from the UNC headquarters developed the same theme:

> For us as Frenchmen the Nation is the union of race and language, a common ideal. The Nation so constituted is the setting from which one can best serve humanity, so that as the country progresses and improves itself, so patriotism becomes worked out. It is these purified forms of patriotism that turn to the League of Nations, less for what it is than for what it should be.[14]

Nation and Humanity

By a logical sequence, as illustrated in these texts, enlightened patriotism is indissoluble from a love of humanity. The extensively quoted article from the *Mutilé du Limousin* discusses this intimate union at length, but the pairing of patriotism and love of humanity occurs particularly frequently.

'We would be serving at the same time the cause of both the nation and of humanity', declared a militant UF in the Pas-de-Calais with reference to November 11,[15] while the UNC concluded one of its core texts, the Wagram Manifesto, with this exhortation:

> Once again, let us do our best by the Nation and by Humanity.[16]

From the linguistic point of view, this association is reinforced by second-hand adjectives. France is 'a human nation,[17] our patriotism is human'.[18] For the left, 'Humanitarian' ideas are synonymous with good patriotism. Another leader of the Pas-de-Calais UF insisted thus on 'refusing our moral support and aid to all those who would make themselves the champions of chauvinistic ideas without rhyme or reason except for vainglory and to the detriment of humanitarian ideas'.[19]

On the right, on the other hand, the opposition was reversed and the adjective 'humanitarian' became pejorative: to the 'pages of glory' (and not 'vainglory') are opposed the 'treaties of humanitarian morale'.[20] But this is an exception: in general the union of the two loves, that of Nation and that of Humanity, is found everywhere.

This is incontestably the enduring legacy of the republican primary school from the early days of the century. The patriotism of Belle Epoque textbooks was no longer naively revisionist: as Jacques and Mona Ozouf have shown, it was a defensive and tolerant patriotism. The right, indeed, made this a subject of complaint against the lay schools, as can be seen after 1908 in the celebrated dispute over patriotism in schools.

The veterans' patriotism was acquired in the Republic's primary schools. I cannot resist the pleasure of quoting here Léon Bourgeois' circular on the teaching of history in schools, for it displays, already fully formed, the characteristic lexical structure of the patriotism of the left:

> The cultivation of national feeling is a delicate matter. Above all the natural love of one's own nation must be reinforced, the instinct must be rationalised and enlightened, but in France, on pain of a lapse of our spirit, we must neither forget the individual in the citizen nor undermine the importance of humanity to the apparent benefit of our nation. . . . It is part of our essential French nature to love humanity and to serve it.[21]

Half a century later Henri Pichot used the same terms to define the mission of schools, in the last article he published before the war: it seemed to him that Edouard Herriot had posed, to a Geneva commission,

> . . . the true problem in asking himself whether university education in every country should be simply national or simultaneously national and human.
>
> This topic, still debated . . . should be permanently present in the sense of a general humanism of national character.
>
> Such words appear self-contradictory; yes, if you place the nation – and worse still the race or the State – in opposition to humanity: no, if you think that the man who is established in his country and his nation should let his heart expand to the world and open his mind liberally to human diversity.
>
> This is the richly national and unreservedly human education that should be offered to all free nations.
>
> . . . French schools should above all teach France, giving each French child an understanding of it. France is not an abstraction, it is a reality. It is from the national community that the citizen draws the constituent and permanent elements of his life in all its aspects. And further, a society cannot perpetuate itself without sustaining its own education.

We have this good fortune, I would say this happiness, that we need not fear to fail humanity by being fully French.

This is why – and I speak as one who has spent his life in the service of education – schools do not fear to make of us the Frenchmen of today: this is how they will give France its men.[22]

This republican form of patriotism which expanded in limitless love for the entire human race is not however entirely innocent. It conceals in fact a subtle national pride and disguises an immense affirmation of the superiority of France over other nations.

France, Soldier of the Ideal

Such enlightened patriotism seemed incapable of mean ideals. It banned national pride. It rejected the admission that France went to war, among other reasons, for Alsace-Lorraine. It maintained on the contrary that she was not pursuing any objectives in her own interest: she fought solely against German militarism and imperialism. Barbusse, for example, did not exclude

the will to conquer Germany . . . because Germany is the strongest expression of dictatorial and unrestrained militarism [but that is] the only reason why she must be conquered.

Others claim that to march towards death and sacrifice one's life one must be driven by a narrow patriotism, or intoxicated by hatred of a race. No. A high promise of ultimate progress is a better stimulus for true men to shed their blood. We who fought as Frenchmen, and above all as men, we can say proudly that we are the living proof.[23]

'We who fought as Frenchmen'! There could be no better claim for France at war than the investiture of humanity's great moral interests. War does not set two nations in opposition on the grounds of equality but on the grounds of chauvinistic militarism and imperialism on the one hand and Right, Justice and Liberty on the other. In the veterans' ideology the war of 1914 thus appears as the last of the Revolutionary wars.

This thesis appears widely, on the right as well as on the left. For René Cassin,* for example, 11 November commemorates the liberation not only of the troops or of Alsace-Lorraine, but of the world:

---

*René Cassin was a professor of law in the University of Paris, and a member of the French delegation to the League of Nations in Geneva. During the Second World War, he was one of the first companions of General de Gaulle in London and was appointed after the war to one of the highest positions in the French civil service, the chair of the Conseil d'Etat.

Finally, liberation of the world, victorious over a monstrous enterprise of oppression conceived and conducted by racial imperialism and pride.

If July 14 is for France and many other nations the symbol of freedoms won by citizens, November 11 marks the crumbling of tyrannical militarism under the combined efforts of free nations.[24]

The classic theme of France at the service of Right, Justice and Liberty reappears, already expressed powerfully, in the order of the day of the *Mutilés du Loiret* for 11 November 1922 (as above, pp. 60–61) or, to quote the phrases current in all minds, Jouhaux's 'We shall be the soldiers of Liberty' spoken over the tomb of Jaurès, or Clemenceau's famous 'France, yesterday warrior of God, today warrior of Humanity, will always be the warrior of the Ideal', announcing the Armistice in the Chamber of Deputies.

So predominant was the veterans' clear conscience that some took it upon themselves to suggest seriously to the Germans that they should adopt 11 November as their national holiday!

The defeated powers, and Germany in particular, should see in this date of November 11 the opening of a new era and the disappearance of a régime which gradually brought them to disaster. It is their July 14 that the free German, truly enamoured of the republican régime which he has adopted, should celebrate on November 11.[25]

Forgetting that in the aftermath of the defeat of 1870 the French had felt well and truly vanquished, even though the republican ideology thrust responsibility for the fatal war on to the Emperor, the veterans never stopped asserting the guilt of imperial Germany for unleashing the war, and they naively thought that the Germans would transmit this on to Wilhelm II,

that emperor whom the civilised nations had indicted for supreme offence against international equity and the sacred force of treaties.[26]

From the beginning to the end of the period, and from the UF to the UNC, the sincere assertion of German guilt and French innocence was uninterrupted. The finest anecdote I can offer is reported by Pichot himself. It was in December 1934, at the time of rapprochement between the French veterans and those of Nazi Germany. Pichot had invited to lunch Oberlindover – the Führer of the National-Socialist veterans – with Ribbentrop and Abetz, and three friends of his own. At the end of the meal he evoked the conditions of rapprochement between France and Germany, and spoke of 'moral reparations'. With candour he suggested that the Germans should recognise that they had been wrong to make war on the French, and then the two nations could become friends. Ribbentrop responded drily: 'If that's so, we will meet again in five years' time'.[27]

France's absolute innocence of implication in the war, proclaimed unanimously by veteran thinking, entailed two highly significant assertions. The first was that international politics is a matter of moral judgement. For them, there were no doubts: there existed a morality of relationships between nations, which was the same as the morality regulating relationships between individuals. Pichot, for example, moved entirely naturally from French innocence to this idea in his speech to the 1922 UF conference in Clermont-Ferrand, which had wide repercussions:

> The war of 1914 was truly the struggle of intelligence against brute strength, of freedom against domination. It was the struggle of democracy against imperialism and militarism, the struggles of nations who are capable of living through ideas against those who live only through their stomachs. There is a morality of nations just as there is a morality of men, or rather higher than men, individuals or nations, there is the morality which is not only respect for man but respect for thought, intelligence, which are man's whole being. . . .
>
> Liberty, justice, truth, citizenship, peace, all these are enduring and tempering qualities.[28]

This is indeed the antithesis of *realpolitik*.

The second statement is an unconscious but breathtaking presumption. It assumes that France incarnates precisely that moral ideal which all nations should obey. It is *the nation* of right, or, to take up again a text of René Cassin, the only nation that symbolises Right on earth, as the Indian delegate at Geneva had remarked.[29]

France is the beacon which should guide all other nations, the 'animator of a better humanity.'[30] Her superiority is of a moral, not material, order. She belongs to the domain of ideas, not of instinct or brute force. This is the area of 'The Marseillaise of Peace', quoted by *Le Mutilé du Limousin*. If Lamartine can say simultaneously 'My country lies wherever France is radiant' and 'Each thinking man is fellow citizen with me/Truth is my country', it is because in his eyes France embodies humanity's highest values: intelligence and the law. In this way she created between herself and all other nations a gulf deeper than the divergence of interests: by placing herself on the side of civilisation she dismissed them to the side of barbarity.

A speech by a UNC leader summarised accurately the essence of these patriotic pretensions to an intellectual and moral superiority which formed the basis of a mission to civilise:

> The wish to ignore other lands in one's life is a fault, a danger and even, in real terms, an absurdity.
>
> This means that our patriotism will not be narrow or selfish, or proud, or full of hatred.
>
> But we retain the right to love our Country and to affirm it. We owe this to her for everything we have received from her.

Then followed a development which expressed all the satisfaction of being French: intelligence, boldness, resourcefulness, sensitivity, France's rich and fertile soil, her workers and craftsmen. The writer went on to evoke France's eastern frontiers and all that they consumed in blood, to conclude (I quote the final part of the speech, to its end):

> France will never call upon her sons to form a frontier nation. She will never make them believe that their destiny is to conquer and to dominate. She will not magnify brute Strength to them.
>
> She will say that the greatest nation is the one that attracts the respect of the world, through the generosity of its actions, through the support it gives to the weak, through the defence of Justice.
>
> She will recall that our tradition has made us protectors of the oppressed and redressers of wrongs, and that our only conquests should be those of intelligence and affection.
>
> She will add: 'Do not seek to destroy, but let your efforts go to relieve human distress'.
>
> She will not offer a Moltke or a Bismarck as models, but she will tell them: 'Seek out the soul of a Pascal among the peaks. Follow the measured teachings of a Descartes. Go, like Doumer or Lyautey, bear civilisation and well-being, culture and progress across the seas. Take pride in that glory alone because it is pure and radiant'.
>
> And it is still by listening to the voice of France that we will work best for the happiness of Humanity.[31]

The Nation of Rights

Through frequent linkage the republican institutions thus appeared as guarantors of French superiority. That France was a Republic proved to the veterans that it was indeed the land of rights, of justice, and of civilisation. This is why it is so difficult to distinguish France from the Republic. On this point the ex-soldiers assimilated to perfection the lessons learned at the primary schools of their childhood.[32] In veterans' writings the expressions Nation, France, and Republic are often interchangeable, and each can be substituted for the others. The study of iconography confirms the conclusions of linguistics. Among the femi-

nine allegories adorning monuments to the dead, Peace can be identified by her olive branch. In contrast, even the Phrygian cap is insufficient to differentiate a 'Republic' from a 'Nation', when a dying *poilu*
turns his gaze towards her. There are not in fact two distinct figures:
monumental statuary to the dead recognises only republican France or
the French Republic.

One can understand better, therefore, why a UNC journal came to
be quoting Jaurès: it was because he expressed to perfection the French
pride in their feeling of having first, and alone, created a civic order
founded on rights and not on force, a fact of prime significance with the
coming of the Republic:

> As republicans and French socialists, none of us could remain indifferent
> to honour or security, to the prosperity of France; we would not only be
> committing a crime against the nation but a crime against humanity, for
> France, free, great and powerful France, is necessary to humanity.

Note the use in this passage of the repeated parallel nation/France/
humanity.

> It is in France that democracy has reached its most logical form: the
> Republic. If France fell, the reaction would resound round the world.[33]

It was however not sufficient just to describe this patriotism. Why
did it achieve such unanimity after the 1914-18 war? Why did the
patriotism of the republican Left become the common ground of all
veterans?

Culture was a prime reason. I hesitate to employ the notion of
national culture, too close to that of national temperament which has in
the past embraced many clichés. The veterans' approach regarding
patriotism seems to me, however, to be typically French in its ethic. It
blurred the material and concrete aspects of the debate, placing it
immediately on the level of ideas and values. Conflicts of interest, rival-
ries, and bargaining moved to the background, and the eternal verities
were invoked from the very beginning.

This ethic was a major characteristic of the veterans' collective thinking: we will meet it again, even more powerful, in other domains; moreover, it fulfilled a social function and constituted an ideology. It can
also be explained by a complex assembly of historical motives connected
with education within the family and with literary and folk traditions,
as well as the action of diverse cultural or social élites. In particular it
owed much to the primary schools without religious affiliation, and the
moralising to which they gave full rein, in order to prove that by abandoning religion they had not destroyed virtue.

The linking of patriotism in the primary school with that of the veterans is obvious. Education in early twentieth-century schools contrasted barbarous nations with just and reasonable nations. *La Morale à l'école*, by Jules Payot, for example – but one could quote dozens of other texts – taught those who were to fight the 1914 war:

> We Frenchmen, let us be a reasonable and just nation. . . .
> We want our nation to be the most just, the most humane, in a word the most reasonable. We wish France to have a reputation for courtesy and for generosity, which will make her beloved by all nations and will attract the esteem of even hostile nations.[34]

One must admit that the lesson was well learnt. The veterans were not content with repeating what they were taught: they believed it.

To morality, referring back to a long tradition, can be added a second reason, narrower but crucial: victory. The veterans were unaware that their words were those of victors. They did not imagine that they could be interpreted as representing precisely the objective interests of the French nation. They were not aware that the vanquished found their moralising patriotism unbearable because it turned the misfortunes of war into punishment, military inferiority into guilt, and the accident of defeat into a sort of merited fate. Still less did they realise that their insistence on rights and justice between nations could be seen as the best way – for a France which had nothing to gain from arms – to stabilise a situation which was currently in their favour, and to restrain the German desire for revenge by making them guilty.

If the patriotism of the veterans was purified, refined, enlarged and tolerant, it was also replete and smug. The France which harboured no further military, territorial or colonial claims could disdain any considerations of self-interest. She could wish sincerely for peace, justice and rights. This was also for her the best way to preserve her hard-won gains. The victory, of which the veterans speak little, thus (as a background to their morality) sealed the reconciliation of patriotism and pacifism in the cult of Rights.

Notes to Chapter 4

1. Meeting at the 1931 Conference of the Orne Union des mutilés, *Journal des mutilés*, 3 May 1931.

2. *Le Combattant sanglier*, February 1932

3. Jacques Delahoche, *Images de guerre, efforts de paix*, Dinard, the author, 1954, p.93.

4. *Les Nations*, June 1917: 'Pourquoi te bas-tu?'

5. *L'Ancien Combattant*, (ARAC), July 1919.

6. Georges Lebecq, speech at the Wagram gathering, *La Voix du combattant*, 21 October 1933.

7. M. Albert Cruchard, Boutefeu collection.

8. Alain, *Mars*, p.169.

9. *Le Combattant sanglier*, May 1930.

10. M. Henry Durand, Boutefeu collection.

11. *Le Mutilé du Limousin*, (UF, Limoges), November 1930.

12. Paul Galland, *La Voix du combattant*, 21 October 1933.

13. *Le Combattant sanglier*, November 1931.

14. *Le Combattant sanglier*, June 1932.

15. Louis Duvet, *Le Combattant du Pas-de-Calais*, 15 May 1922.

16. *La Voix du combattant*, 21 October 1933.

17. Henri Pichot, report to the 1935 UF conference, in *Les Combattants avaient raison*, Montluçon, 1940.

18. *Les Cahiers du l'UF*, 15 August 1936.

19. Fleury Cresson, *Le Combattant du Pas-de-Calais*, 10 August 1927.

20. Louis Schaepelynck, *Le Poilu du Centre*, November 1926.

21. Circular of 5 July 1890.

22. Henri Pichot, *Les Cahiers de l'UF*, 15 July 1939.

23. Henri Barbusse, article published in *L'Oeuvre* in 1917, reprinted in *Paroles d'un combattant*, Paris, Flammarion, 1920, p.27.

24. *La France mutilée*, 19 November 1922.

25. Duvet, *Le Combattant du Pas-de-Calais*, 15 February 1922.

26. Maurice Robert, *La France mutilée*, 19 November 1922.

27. The anecdote appears in an unpublished text by Pichot, preserved with his papers, entitled 'Et ce fut quand même la guerre' (And even so it was war). We are grateful to Henri Pichot's son, M. Pierre Pichot, for his permission to consult these important papers.

28. *Congrès UF 1922*, pp.421–422.

29. René Cassin, *La France mutilée*, 19 November 1922.

30. Appeal published in *Le Poilu du Centre*, February 1924.

31. Léon Berthier, *La Voix du combattant*, 21 October 1933.

32 'The nation that children should love is, we are assured by the textbooks, France and the Republic' in Jacques and Mona Ozouf, 'Le thème du patriotisme dans les manuels primaires', *Le Mouvement social*, (October-December 1964), pp.3–31.

33. Quoted by *Le Combattant sanglier*, December 1933.

34. Jules Payot, *La Morale à l'école*, Paris, A. Colin, 1907, pp.221–223.

5

Veterans' Politics:
Attitudes and Ethics

Initially it may be difficult to imagine that there could be a specifically 'veteran's' attitude to political matters. Natural enough in matters of foreign policy, where the ex-soldiers' wish for peace was readily understandable, or in certain specific matters such as reform of the code of military law, pensions, or the status of the severely disabled: but that there·might be a particular way in which former *poilus* should approach the political arena was, it appeared, a bold hypothesis. To have taken part in the war was not a qualification for creating policy, and did not appear to establish a particular approach. Further, how could men from all classes of society and all ideological backgrounds agree on the same political preferences?

In fact marked divergences among the veterans were clearly apparent on most specific political questions. Concerning the Cartel of 1924 – as, later, Doumergue's ministry – the societies were divided: there was no unanimity of thought. However the political debate acquired similar forms in all the societies. Before looking at the possible significance of any one theory, we should examine the specifically veterans' approach to political problems.

The Place of Political Debate

For the veterans' associations political debate was not central: it was not the prime purpose of their existence. Although it was extremely important at certain times, notably in 1933–34, the fact that it was subject to clear variations of significance gives it a unique position.

Politics intervened in the life of the societies as a crowning element. It was an order of reality that expanded the debate and raised the level of interest. However legitimate, the defence of rights or specific claims

Notes to Chapter 5 can be found on page 114.

was not of itself sufficient to justify the very existence of the societies in the eyes of their own members. Such objectives were too limited, too materialistic, too inward-looking. By limiting themselves to such matters, members would be open to the justified reproach of pursuing their aims in too limited a manner, denounced by some outside the veterans' movement as mean-minded or worse. All such detractors must be shown that ex-soldiers were by no means greedy parasites; their vision was wider, their thinking more elevated, their concern broader.

Through their discussion of matters of general interest the veterans attained a more elevated and high-minded order of interest, the only one truly worthy of citizens who once saved the nation. For holders of office within the societies this extension of their concern responded to a precise perception of their members' aspirations, in particular of their rural members. In France's villages and small towns the veterans' clubs fulfilled several functions simultaneously. In particular they were a door to the outside world and society as a whole. One could not be fully satisfied, at the end of an annual general meeting or a cantonal conference, without having heard the great problems of the moment raised in ways that were sufficiently pointed and thorough to be interesting, but sufficiently neutral to avoid embarrassment. The officials at *département* level added their encouragement with particular enthusiasm because they felt responsible for shaping public opinion, and saw their mission in educational terms. As the end-product of lay teaching institutions or Catholic instruction they had an educational vocation, and would not consider their task accomplished if they had not helped to extend the instruction and citizenship of their members.

In fact the club officials, with admirable evangelical impulse, organised a proliferation of meetings every year in even the most isolated communities. Local styles of meeting were undoubtedly not politically neutral: in western France the traditional local worthies played a preponderant role and were well accepted despite a touch of paternalism. In more republican areas meetings were more democratic and more respectful of technical formality: but in neither case did any meeting end without discussion of some 'big' question. These rounds of propaganda reached a great number of communes each year, in every *département*. We can follow, for example, those of the Loiret disabled: on winter Sundays, they took in between 80 and 100 local branches. Special meetings were also organised if occasion required; for example, the UNC in Corrège noted very numerous branch meetings after the riots of 6 February 1934, in 1935 in Loiret there were very well-supported meetings on the topic of governmental reform – 150 people present at

Baule, out of 314 electors and 220 in Jargeau out of 603 electors, to hear Pichot speak; but also 200 people in Beaugency and 100 at Outarville, or again 270 in Artenay out of 339 electors, to listen to other departmental officials. And Loiret was by no means an exception.

Remarkable in its scale, the programme of civic instruction undertaken by the societies was equally remarkable in its technicality. The veteran movements' speakers did not hesitate to explain, without distorting simplification and without concessions, systems as complex as the procedures of international arbitration. They distributed simple but precise leaflets by the hundred thousand on governmental reform, analysing in detail the functioning of its institutions, their defects and possible remedies. The UF printed 600,000 copies of *La République des combattants*, a 48-page booklet written by Pichot. The UNC and the FNCR followed suit. Such efforts were indeed ambitious in concept: they involved nothing less than explaining to millions of citizens, mostly country folk of limited education, questions as complex as the difference between constituency voting and proportional representation. What other network of societies, not excluding those linked to political parties, would have been capable at that period of sustaining such debate on such topics throughout the whole of France?

However impressive these efforts, their limitations remain obvious. The clubs could not become wholeheartedly involved without losing members, unless their patient labour of explanation elicited a substantial consensus on limited measures. They took a stand on various unpromising matters such as social policies (family allowances, social security, housing improvements), but took care not to embark on more delicate issues. Analysing problems and assessing difficulties took precedence over proposals and were accompanied by exhortations to exercise civic virtues. The veterans' political approach thus adopted two particular aspects: dissemination of information on the one hand and incitement to citizenship on the other.

Stereotypes of Veterans' Discussion

Civic instruction also undoubtedly took precedence over information: it alone could offer the veterans' movement a range that would be broader, more generous and more high-minded than claims on everyday matters. By stating firmly the moral demands of citizenship and the great principles by which life in society should be regulated, the veterans hoped to offer an example and a lesson that would be of value to all. At the same time they placed themselves in a privileged position, that of the guardians of truth and goodness – the position, in fact, that their patriotism claimed for France in relation to other nations. Just as France was for them the beacon-nation, the instigator of a better form of humanity, so within their own nation the veterans formed a privileged group, the forces of sanity capable of showing the road to well-being and speaking for justice and right. This is what they expected to confirm when they spoke of their 'moral magistrature'.

In such circumstances the specific characteristics of ex-soldiers' pronouncements on politics are more easily understood. Before offering illustrative extracts and considering their true import, we should draw up a brief inventory of the stereotypes imposed by the style of these pronouncements on the actual activities of these groups. In effect there was a code for most of the veteran movements' political statements which may resist attempts at commentary.

The tone of veterans' statements on politics was fundamentally ethical· in style: they aimed to exercise a moral effect on the recipients. They wished to develop their civic virtues and to strengthen their unity, extending beyond antagonisms. For this it was necessary to win over the heart even more than the mind: statements must stir and engage. This function was heavy with consequences both stylistically and in terms of vocabulary.

On the level of style this type of discourse was rhetorical. It made free use of direct speech to the audience, to whom it would frequently issue imperatives, using the imperative voice. It made use of rhetorical questions and emphatic turns of speech (He who ..., it is he who ...). It sought striking phrases. It particularly favoured phrases of binary structure which enabled the speaker to go beyond apparent contradictions, either by immediately restricting an assertion or in juxtaposing two denials or two symmetrical choices.

On the level of vocabulary, this discourse used grand words to indicate grand principles. All 'moral expressions' could appear, for citizenship included the whole range of moral values. Certain expressions, or pairs of expressions, were particularly prevalent – thus the opposition of the general interest and particular interests, the essence of citizenship, of solidarity, fraternity, unity, discipline freely entered into, openness, the alliance of realism and idealism, etc. In short, it drew extensively on the 'common ground' of classic moral rhetoric.

A unifying concept made it possible at the same time to bring together all these principles and give them a specifically 'veteran' label: this was the 'veteran spirit'. This spirit was indefinable: born of the war, it was not present in all ex-soldiers, while some non-veterans did possess it. Its definition varied according to the writer or speaker's whim. For all, however, it was the essence of goodness, of public spirit as it should be, and which must be instilled everywhere.

In the face of the veterans' spirit, the negative form was 'division', the scourge invoked incessantly, for it was a constant threat not only to the nation but to the societies themselves. Division was the product of politics, more precisely of party politics. It came from a spirit that was the precise opposite of the veterans' spirit, being a 'partisanship' which must be scrupulously eliminated from the clubs, political parties and the whole of national life.

Such a discourse thus implied the 'separation into two types of policy'; the despised one of party or partisan politics, which must be avoided, and the favoured, the permitted policy derived from the veterans' spirit, in other words the veterans' policies or, more often, civic activity.

The separation into two types of policy was accompanied by a double claim: in opposition to politicians the veterans laid claim to moral superiority and also to integrity. The claim to superiority was expressed in a vocabulary of spatial terms: they were above party politics, on the peaks, higher, further forward. The claim to integrity was a refusal to compromise: that was not within their remit. They had nothing to do with effective policies, with pragmatic politics that risked compromise. Their political discourse was therefore frequently unrealistic: in order to remain generalised it avoided precise designations. The parties which it discussed remained undefined. The actions it demanded remained imprecise; it identified no concrete objectives, no adversaries, no allies, proposed no imminent realisation. The ethic however insisted on action, and it easily counterbalanced words and deeds. Hence an incantatory call to action: 'To act is everything'.

For this reason the aims of the veterans' movement in the political arena were concealed and it was not easy to perceive them beyond this stereotyped moralising rhetoric. Before identifying them and suggesting an interpretation, it therefore seems essential to get used to this apparently static and meaningless vocabulary. The veterans' political discourse seems empty because its function excludes explicit conclusions; but it requires only understanding of how it operated for it to become clear.

Moral Rhetoric

Plentiful examples are more useful than lengthy comment. First, the end of two major addresses launching the themes of the veterans' spirit and civic activity: Pichot's speech to the 1922 UF conference in

Clermont-Ferrand and Ernest Pezet's speech to the 1923 UNC conference in Vichy. The literary genre of the major conference speech clearly entails a rhetorical style.

Pichot first:

> The veterans' spirit is nothing other than the French and human spirit as it has developed with time. What we have been saying offers nothing new, nothing startling, nothing original, nothing unexpected. Did we really need the war for French people worthy of the name to love and serve liberty, justice, truth, their nation, peace? Undoubtedly not. But the French of pre-war days had let their thinking become clouded, and the war restored to all these ancient traditional virtues their meaning and their value. The war thus revealed nothing new, except that the essential value of individuals and of nations does not change, and that history repeats itself. The same errors produce the same disasters; the same virtues produce the same renewals.
>
> No, ex-soldiers are not exceptional men. The ex-soldiers' ideas are ancient ideas; the ex-soldiers' feelings are ancient feelings. But these ideas, these truths and these feelings need to live through humankind. The moment they are abandoned, the moment they are denied, the moment they are forgotten, the moment they are insulted, the moment they are trampled under foot, it is as if they were destroyed. But the moment they are recognised, the moment they are considered, the moment they are loved, it is as if they were being created. . . .
>
> Our action is not dying away. It is only beginning.
>
> Beyond the sacred interests of the people which it is our duty to defend, there remain, eternal and imperishable, the interests of the cause for which we have struggled and for which so many men have died.
>
> It is to defence, in the service of the human concept to which we all give what is best within us: the defence of our beliefs and faiths, our convictions, our ardour and the radiant strength of our downtrodden bodies.
>
> Indeed, we must understand clearly that if the men of the war yield and give way [note the lack of precision] France and the world will founder into selfishness, baseness and anarchy. The combined strength of all our wills would not be excessive, to save them a second time.
>
> Men of war, let us be men of peace, let us be the soldiers of liberty, the soldiers of justice, the soldiers of truth, the soldiers of humanity. For generations will pass away, nations will pass away, riches, honour and glory will pass away; but liberty, and justice, and truth will not pass away.
>
> And the spirit, despite the ragings of mankind, will reign over the world.[1]

This passage explicitly asserts the identity of the veterans' spirit and eternal morality, as in the pairing French/human noted in the preceding chapter. The style is necessarily rhetorical, with notable cadences of repetition (the moment they . . . the moment they . . . the moment they . . .;

will pass away . . . will pass away . . . will pass away . . .). The moral vocabulary is very rich (selfishness, baseness, errors, virtues, etc.). Finally, Pichot addresses his public directly but does not separate himself from them: he uses the imperative, but in the first person plural: let us be men of peace, let us be the soldiers of liberty.

Ernest Pezet whips up his audience more vigorously, and his appeal to moral effort takes on the accents of an appeal to virility:

> One of our greatest comrades, a magnificent war writer, Jean des Vignes Rouges, whom I have already quoted, has written some lines which I offer in conclusion for your consideration:
>
> On the day when distinguished people, men and women, step forward into the arena and address as rulers the crowds who prance about on dance-floors or who sit back in idleness – on that day we will embark on the new ages of which noble minds are dreaming. . . .
>
> The ex-soldiers, their sons, and all the spiritual heirs of our dead are noble cells that still survive amid the amorphous mass of the post-war population; if they die or if they abdicate, nothing would remain but a mob without a soul, a great mindless beast dragging itself across French soil. An unbearable prospect! . . .
>
> You must be leaders, an ardent purpose to touch your souls, to draw them up noble and dominant above this post-war crowd.
>
> Oh, don't mistake me: if it were only a matter of stirring the coarse ambitions of vulgar indulgence, my voice would remain unheard; but you are men refined by the sufferings of war and so much the better if my words unleash in your hearts the passion to dominate, for what will triumph with you will be everything that is most worthy to be made law.
>
> Comrades! Stand up and take command! For you the war was the great mystic redemption that justifies your right and guarantees the purity of your conscience.
>
> He who has risked death for the Nation in the fierce light of battle has no need to hide when he seeks to complete his task – by assuming the trials of leadership.
>
> My masterful comrades, make your decision.[12]

Such phrases may be disturbing: the appeal to dominate is reminiscent, in 1923, of Mussolini. Pezet, however, was a Christian-Democrat and was never to turn to Fascism. Here he has let himself be carried away by the literary style of the major conference speech, and has chosen words which make the right sound to inspire a standing ovation at the close. Neither his text nor Pichot's can be understood outside the cultural context where eloquence is valued in the abstract. Two years later Pezet himself was to contribute to the foundation of the DRAC public speaking competition, when advocates of the meetings felt it important to coach Catholic school pupils in the art of public oratory.

An Ethic for Action

Texts for publication as articles were however not much less rhetorical than these speeches. The officials of the veterans' movement wrote as they spoke in public, and their style favoured oratorical phrasing, particularly when concluding. Without excessive quotation, it is worth showing the styles most frequently favoured. First there was emphasis, achieved by recourse to what rhetoricians refer to as 'presentational' phrases, of the type 'It is x that is . . .'. Ernest Pezet once more provides an example, using four presentational phrases in a row and impressive-sounding but undefined objectives:

> The veterans expect something 'new', new in concept, will, sincerity, feeling. The 'veteran spirit' is little concerned with the classifications, habits, conventions and proposals of the political parties! It is not 'politics' that they want: we cannot state this too often.
>
> It is not parties that they wish to serve, nor a party that they wish to form.
>
> It is a conquest of 'the public spirit' that 'the veteran spirit' should undertake.
>
> It is an operation of 'public welfare' as well as an operation of defence and personal security that must be accomplished with the vigour, impartiality, and probity worthy, I must repeat, of a 'Committee of Public Welfare'.
>
> This is the attitude of mind.
>
> There must be ideas, a master plan: obviously. The circumstances for action must be identified: agreed.
>
> We will return to this. But these outlines, this precise expression of our 'attitude of mind' were the first essential.
>
> Comrades of all parties – except for those which blaspheme against the Nation, Justice or Freedom – will understand these directions. All can share in this 'attitude of mind', this 'veterans' spirit'.[3]

This text underlines the spirit of veterans: its opposition to party politics, its assumed moral vocation (the conquest of the public mind), and its universality. These same traits appear from the pen of Humbert Isaac, this time with slightly different stylistic usage, particularly rhetorical questions, the claim to a higher plane, and the lack of precise definition:

> Depending on local conditions our groups, our branches, our members can operate as they wish in the *départements* to achieve the victory of our will, to see France *united, restored, repopulated, prosperous, grateful* to those who saved her, assured of her *security* in a world that is gradually being *paci-*

fied. This is what all French people can and should want: this is not being 'political' in the usual sense of the word, it is to rise above politics, stripping away what does not belong to it; it is to float above the parties when all, unless they make a mockery of their nation, would come together in this sphere.

It would perhaps frustrate certain ambitions ready for the challenge, like those content to remain behind on the home front while we were out there. Is it not still our duty? Are we not assured of success if we can will it?

Is it not free from risk, if we are wise enough not to exceed the textbook concepts, of which the consequences will gradually become sufficiently clear, if we can avoid offending politicians and parties, or admitting to our Committees any who are not proven men, or encouraging or tolerating manoeuvrings among ourselves, whether external or internal, which would end in creating a springboard for men of ambition?

. . . Comrades of the UNC, almost everywhere you will surely make up your minds to take your place in the action that will gradually evolve everywhere, whatever you do, with or without you, because everywhere the veterans' spirit is re-emerging from its somewhat relaxed state. You will help to ensure round you, among our comrades and among those whom the war did not call to arms, that *awakening of conscience* that must assure the welfare of the nation. With prudence but without needless timidity, and shoulder to shoulder like élite troops, you will accomplish the duty which we feel to be incumbent upon us.[4]

This moralising speech is identified by more than its tricks of rhetorical style. It deliberately adopts a binary structure to define the moral ideal that it proposes, whether opposing virtue and vice or specifying a quality by proscribing its excess. Here, with added italics to emphasise the opposition of expressions, is an example of the first procedure:

> The voice of the Veterans has spoken.
>
> It demands that *competence* should replace *favouritism*, that *probity* should replace *'cushy'* jobs, that *work* should replace *idleness*, that *republican order* should displace *anarchy*, that *system* should dispel *caprice*, that *solidarity of goodwill* should suppress *divisive differences*, that *trusting cooperation* should drive out *the class struggle*, that *love*, in fact, should destroy *hatred.*[5]

This is a skillful presentation, for it leaves any potential dissenter without a line to pursue. In effect, if he refuses his support, the speech places him among the vices listed. If he questions the system he can be reproached with being capricious. From the outset the challenger is condemned by the pejorative nature of the setting.

The other process follows a different aim: this time it is not a matter of reducing the disputant to an unfavourable defensive position but to render contradiction impossible by presenting the argument in a very general form which also refutes any possible objections in advance. The best example would seem to be this appeal to the UNC in the aftermath of 6 February 1934:

> The voice of the UNC is the voice of the Nation itself.
> The Nation is republican.
> The Nation is in favour of authority, and against autocracy.
> The Nation is national, it is not nationalist.
> The Nation is peaceful, it is not pacifist.
> The Nation is democratic, it is not demagogic.
> The Nation is social, it is not socialist.
> The Nation loves its army, guardian of its safety, it is not militaristic.
> The Nation is tolerant and liberal, it detests sectarians.
> The Nation is weary of chatterers, it is eager for action.
> The Nation is honest and healthy, it demands justice.
> The Nation blends together in single love the hearth of the Family and that of the Motherland.
> The Nation wishes to be healed. It can be. It must be.
> Frenchmen, French women,
> Your pressing duty is not to carry on in isolation.
> Join, and encourage others to join – *Action Combattante*.[6]

In this example the purpose is more political than ethical, and the text tends to the right. But the process is familiar. It can be seen particularly in the exhortations addressed to the young, by the UNC as well as by the UF, and in which one can expect to find some sort of resume of the veterans' morality. The following text comes from Léon Viala, one of the UF leaders:

> The UF should be in the front rank . . . calling for the maintenance of order and reminding certain categories of citizens that the most sacred rights do not exclude certain duties; to appeal to the common sense of those who have difficulty in accepting inevitable social changes. . . .
>
> I would like to see a beginning to the progressive substitution of the *young* for the *old* so that a fair balance may be established between the careful wisdom of the one and the youthful ardour of the other, so that the wise counsel of the 'old' may aid the inexperience of the 'young'.
>
> My final word, in the dawn of this new year, will again be to the *young*: be bold within reason, be men of action and not restless souls, be ambitious but not impulsive, remember your responsibilities as well as your rights; be good French citizens; be men.[7]

The familiar pairing is in evidence again here – French/men – and the rhetorical tricks already noted, such as the direct imperative.

Presentational phrases reappear elsewhere (It is not . . . to . . .) and the emphatic use of moral obligation reinforcing the imperative, as in this *Epistle to Youth* by Aimé Goudaert, Chairman of the Nord branch of the UNC:

> It is not taking action, to complain. It is not taking action to create use-less agitation.
>
> *It is not enough to do good, you must do better. . . .*
>
> Perpetuate the spirit of the generation of fire. Be tolerant, be united above party and social class. Join us in fighting selfishness, the public enemy which silences the voice of morality and which led us into the depths where we now find ourselves. Always behave like Frenchmen. Behave towards your elders with courtesy but without duplicity, with openness but without harshness, with compliance but without flattery, with regard but without constraint. . . .
>
> The time for rest is past, for sleep is the image of death. You must have the courage to face the risks.
>
> Each one of us must bring what he can give, and you must accept freely, joyously, wholly, the discipline that we ask of you for our programme of domestic, social and national renewal.[8]

These two texts do not display identical political leanings. In certain themes, such as domestic renewal, the UNC text veers to the right, while in 1937, to stress with Léon Viala the responsibilities that accompany the most sacred of rights – i.e., property – is an argument leaning towards the *Front populaire*, but in these two cases the same code served to formulate two different political messages. In both there is undefined action – opposed to agitation – and a call for unity. On both sides the same imperatives, the same verbs underlining moral obligation (we must) the same pairing rhythms (openness without harshness, ambition without impulsiveness). For anyone unfamiliar with this specific language, the differences are lost and only the similarities remain in the memory.

The precise language of the veterans must therefore be examined with great care for, although they do not all say exactly the same thing, the fact that they employ a common code – and the structure of this code – is by no means mere insignificant coincidence.

The Veterans' Spirit

One of the pivotal points of this language is the veterans' spirit, already encountered in several guises. The existence of a unique spirit born of the war is indeed the proposition underlying the whole veteran discourse, both political and ethical. Before describing this spirit – which is the subject of various books[9] – it must be stated, first, that it existed and, second, that it united ex-soldiers. Thus for this unnamed contributor from Seine-Inférieure, who signed the article with his veteran's card number:

> They are wrong (those who see us divided), for they are ignorant of what unites us, of what moves us, of what adds to our number: the veterans' spirit is indefinable, born amid the hardships of war, a feeling of love and goodness recreated daily by the pleasure of having improved the life of one of yesterday's friends.
>
> The veterans' spirit is the basis for our hope, everywhere the same, it inspires countless groups![10]

That there was a veterans' spirit could not be questioned, even on the extreme left. Vaillant-Couturier refused to base a policy on this spirit, but he did not question its existence:

> A veterans' spirit exists, that is true. A spirit which must be cultivated, upheld, a spirit of mutual aid, of solidarity, acquired in common wretchedness, a spirit which above all fed on the horror of battle and the scorn of those who contemplated it.[11]

As to a precise definition of this spirit, that is another matter. The innumerable texts that make the attempt, in a few lines or a few pages, waver between two forms of presentation: the stereotype of the *poilu* character on the one hand and the universal principles of morality on the other.

Realism and Frankness

A primary set of definitions bases the veterans' spirit on habits acquired in the trenches: the horror of 'eye-wash' created a love of realism, the severity of the living conditions produced a certain harshness. The war was a school of realism, of unselfishness and of resolution. Hence the stereotype of the veteran, a man who does not burden himself with oratorical caution, who looks things straight in the eye, with common sense, who is not proud, who detests privilege and practices mutual help. Rough honesty, realism, devotion, resolution and solidarity thus make up a composite portrait, repeated on all sides. Here for example the chairman of the Ardennes UNC introduces his branch to a new *préfet*, using the familiar 'nation/humanity' pairing and other persuasive rhetoric:

> We are not concerned with politics. Or rather, we know only one form of

politics: that which will make France the greatest and most humane of nations.

'Above and beyond all parties' is not an empty formula for us; here, you can understand this; we consist of men from all points of the political compass. And so it has been since 1919.

It is because we are true veterans, plain-spoken but loyal-hearted, and because we have a common ideal, the prosperity of the nation.

In combining together we have rejected nothing of our true selves, of our political individuality; but, as in the trenches, we have learned to know ourselves and to love each other, we know how to respect in others what we wish them to respect in us.

This mutual respect of consciences is our strength and makes us indestructible as a body.

We are the Boars, but as such, our rough hides conceal a particularly sensitive heart.[12]

This group's very name summarises this stereotype of the ex-soldier: 'The Ardennes Boars'.

That there was nothing unusual in this can be confirmed by two more texts. The first comes from the administrative director of the UNC, Hubert-Aubert:

The veterans are realists. They are wary – as of shells – of all humbugs, of all fanatics, of those who hide their lack of thought and action beneath aggressive words and who anaesthetise opinion, as well as of those who, to achieve their aims better and quicker, offer their neighbours a distant planet to admire . . . that will never be attained. . . .

The *poilus* know how slow is victory, but they know too that with perseverance it is possible to break down resistance.[13]

The second example, from an anonymous member of ARAC in 1919, also avoids specificity:

We have suffered too much from 'eye-wash' to practice it ourselves. For more than four years we were the victims of the fine talkers with hollow phrases who carried on the war in a disgraceful way.

For that very reason we do not claim recompense in words. We will move on to deeds.

We will not use our ambition to prepare a vast and complex programme. We are realists: we know exactly where we are in the present situation; we examine its immediate consequences and distant repercussions coolly. Tomorrow we will make demands, we will insist that people adopt the solution that we think best, because it is the most equitable.[14]

This continuing thread of the veterans' spirit which stresses rough openness and realism, like determination, is often accompanied by powerful language: do not forget the 'My masterful comrades, decide' of Ernest Pezet. This is a slope down which the veterans' style of speech occasionally let itself slide, in its wish to galvanise its audience. ARAC itself occasionally yielded to it, as seen in this newspaper paragraph set in bold type, in the August 1919 issue of *Ancien Combattant*:

> Ex-soldier, you must be a new man.
> During the war you obeyed, in time of Peace you alone should command.
> You saved everything, the nation, both people and possessions. You alone have nothing. Reclaim your place in the sun.
> Be aware. Be free.
> Let us group ourselves together. Let us be a united bloc, united by strong discipline but freely accepted.

Note the citizen-stereotype of discipline freely accepted, general throughout the veterans' world.

The Veterans' Virtues

The second set of definitions identifies the ex-soldiers' spirit with public spirit as it should be. It answers the same purpose, but by other means. Defining matters by their origins guaranteed the unity of the veterans: forged by the same experiences, they share the same soul. Definitions by means of universal morality certainly ensured unity among them, but expanded to include all good citizens. The former tended to exclude non-combatants but the second, in contrast, tended to include them.

> The veterans' spirit is the spirit of those who learned or relearned a certain set of virtues in the harsh school of war, such as acceptance of sacrifice, self-denial, the need to subordinate individual interests to general interests, devotion of one to all, active and purposeful solidarity, fraternity, or better still, brotherly love, with in addition a taste for action and the true meaning of progress.
>
> There are entirely genuine veterans who have never possessed this spirit. There are others who, back in everyday civilian life, have lost it in the atmosphere of a sick society subject to the drive of more or less legitimate ambitions to satisfy more or less high-minded appetites. Judgement does not lie in our hands. We wish to work with our former companions who feel the inspiration of the veterans' spirit and even with those who, despite not having taken part in the war like us and with us, have been infused with the power of this spirit which warms their energies and their generosity.[15]

According to this approach, the war did not create a genuinely new spirit: it revived the importance of traditional virtues. This is what Pichot said in his speech to the Clermont-Ferrand conference quoted above. This is what he repeated in an article reproduced in a publicity leaflet:

> We are convinced . . . that the veterans' spirit is not dead, that the men who went to war have kept faith with the old days. Alas, the war did not offer any genuine revelations; it restored meaning and vigour to forgotten truths; it reminded the French of the power of national instinct; it proved once more the need for discipline and the value of social meaning. It estab-lished the superiority of action, by which we mean considered action, over speech-making and agitation. It proved that nothing can be achieved except in the name of a doctrine 'hrough a system, in a word through a policy. It made clear above all that mutual brotherhood and respect are possible beyond all kinds of divergence and opposition. It has revived in veterans' minds the love of great ideas so often tarnished and corrupted by those who made use of them instead of serving them.[16]

In this more technical review article the style is less rhetorical than usual, although the ideas remain those of the Clermont conference.

Most texts, however, brought the two definitions together and drew from them, as the lesson taught by war, moral principles broad enough to allow most people to support them. Here for example is one of the administrators of the Pas-de-Calais UF:

> A federation of ex-soldiers unites men of widely-varying attitudes, social circumstances, beliefs and ideas, but who have moulded a new spirit in the melting pot of war, referred to by José Germain as the veterans' spirit. It is this spirit which shapes the essence of our Federations: the spirit of justice, the spirit of goodness, the spirit of tolerance, the spirit of sacrifice. Only other veterans have lived closer to death, or for so long. The near approach of death makes men wiser and better. Wiser, for in its presence man feels small and seeks round him the support he needs to avoid being drawn into the abyss suddenly opening at his feet. Better, for in its presence he observes the sterility of the hatred that divides mankind. In the face of death, love can be seen as the source of life. Ex-soldiers have turned their back on death and opened their arms wide to love. Love for their own people, love for their companions in wretchedness, love of their country. Whether they are religious believers or free thinkers, whether they are men of the right or the left, whether they are rich or poor, they are always, whether they wish it or not, dominated by this feeling of love which unites men who fought in the war and which engenders a spirit of justice and goodness.[17]

This veteran's sincerely expressed attitude is used elsewhere as a pre-text for more suspect oratorical developments, as in the case of José Germain referred to above, not because he invented the veterans' spirit, but because he devoted a resounding speech to it in the Pas-de-Calais, described in the local UF journal in the following terms:

With rare talent, with that faith of the Artois *poilu* defining this spirit born out of the war, José Germain developed his theme along the following twelve points:

1. The Veteran is attached to the country which he saved because he suffered for it.
2. He is a man of peace because he knows a lot about war.
3. He knows the meaning of action and distrusts mere speech-makers.
4. Realistic in his idealism, he is not open to dangerous ideology.
5. He is driven by hatred of disorder.
6. He is constructive, through hatred of the destruction of war.
7. He is hostile to lies and detests 'eye-wash'.
8. He has a feeling for the general interest to which he submits his own interest.
9. He has a liking for accepted authority and discipline.
10. With his experience of solidarity, he possesses team spirit.
11. As a strong supporter of political and religious tolerance he is not subject to social hatred.
12. Finally, he is capable of accepting responsibility.

This is a masterpiece of clarity. The written word is incapable of rendering an account worthy of such a distinguished speech, and moreover these ideas are of such clarity and precision that this summary of the conference may be regarded as the Gospel of the Veterans.[18]

Elsewhere it is impossible to dissociate rhetorical amplification from sincere belief. Georges Pineau believed in the veterans' spirit while simultaneously attributing uncertain consequences to it.

> War achieved the miracle of destroying selfishness. Each man in that huge army felt so small, so abandoned, so anonymous, that he depended on the support of his companions. What yesterday appeared a cause for action was no longer important. What was the point of making plans when no one knew if they would live to see tomorrow? The shadow of death filled every mind and the constant threat of danger sustained in everyone the feeling of vital solidarity.
>
> It was no longer a matter of 'living one's life' at the expense of others, but of living honestly, like a good fellow, in the present moment which might be one's last.

Hitherto the analysis is backed by war experiences and rings reasonably true. But now comes a touch of ideological interpretation:

> War brought hearts and minds closer together. Detached from all material cares, purified through suffering, men's minds were fired with trembling enthusiasm for this fine feeling of friendship. In those weary ill-treated bodies quivered souls of flame.
>
> And all those men who were the great victims of hatred loved each other like brothers.

The veterans' spirit – the common soul of the generation of fire – is thus primarily the spirit of brotherhood. It is also the spirit of truth: in the face of death the mask falls away, men stop acting.

It is the spirit of peace which as well as hatred of war between nations, of civil war and of quarrels between parties and classes, includes the profound wish to meet each other, to understand and esteem each other. It is the spirit of discipline, each citizen working in his place for the well-being of all, the general interest taking priority over the individual interest. It is the spirit of freedom that assures for each individual the right to act and think as he wishes. It is the spirit of citizenship, with all members of the city-state taking a generous interest, according to their means, in public affairs.

Already nine years have passed.

Pessimists assert that the veterans' spirit has melted away in the multiplicity of concerns of the post-war period. Time – that pitiless grave-digger of the dearest memories – has dispelled memories of the painful past.

Note the allusion, confirming the comments of Chapter 1, concerning the evolution of recollection. This was written in 1927!

And each one has resumed his hideous former expression.
This is not so.

When you meet the Men who went to War, you perceive quickly that their soldierly spirit still lives intensely within them. No! Men do not forget.

Speak to the veterans, tell them the truth directly, which politicians refuse to hear, evoke memories of the war, do not mince words, and you will see them tremble and recover themselves.

Thus it is to you, leaders and comrades of the UNC, that I turn finally, for it is you who must maintain the veterans' spirit. Militants in great cities or in villages, our duty is to preach the word tirelessly of the coming together of hearts and to give, ourselves, the example of honest lives that the veterans' spirit demands in every action.[19]

The Veterans' Spirit

Many more quotations are available. Better, however, to raise the question of the significance of the 'veterans' spirit' stereotype. Four elements are apparent.

First, these arguments include an element of truth. On certain points the war does indeed seem to have modified behaviour and thinking. It was not the school of brotherhood that the ex-soldiers describe, but all experienced there moments of intense brotherly emotion. Their horror of 'eye-wash' is indisputable. Similarly, it is true that communal life taught Catholics and non-believers to know each other better, to honour each other, and to respect each other. Their squabbles of the early part of the century came to be seen as pointless and artificial. For

the veterans the religious question belonged to a lost past, and lay teachers lived on good terms in their ranks with ecclesiastics. This fact struck
the *préfet* as sufficiently important for him to narrate a revealing incident of this new spirit at the UF conference in Orleans in 1919.

> Father Matteudi then appealed to the union to remain as strong in peace
> as it had been during the war. A lay teacher proclaimed that the gulf separat-
> ing state teachers from religious teachers no longer existed. Cordial hand-
> shakes with Father Matteudi underlined [sic] this statement.[20]

The war marked more than the end of the anti-Dreyfus type of
patriotism, à la Déroulède or Barrès. For the veterans it also marked the
end of anticlericalism à la Combes.

Similarly, the veterans' cliché concerning authority and discipline is
not totally without foundation. A sound observer, Georges Bonnet,
observed this as early as 1917. He quoted with approval Georges de
Tarde:

> The France of 1914-1917 is more truly democratic than ever before, and
> she is in love with command. . . .
> On the one hand, the prestige of intelligence and will, the need for leaders
> and sound government, energetic and full of resolution – on the other hand
> a passionate feeling for social justice – these are the two ends of the chain.

And he confirmed, on his own account:

> The wishes of the soldiers should be well understood: in future they want
> leaders of true merit capable of deliberately exercising necessary authority
> but still without encroaching on liberties acquired and more deserved than
> ever.[21]

It seemed, in fact, that the pressure of war conditions brought a new
appreciation of the problems of command, authority being obviously
necessary although authoritarianism was unacceptable.

Reference to the veterans' spirit was however not only an echo of
actual experience. A second element was the wish to give meaning to
the war, even when it had been experienced as absurd butchery and useless massacre. To assert the existence of the veterans' spirit was to assert
that the war was not totally pointless. As well as material destruction
and death it had a message for those who had taken part in it. This is
the persistently recurrent theme of the 'lessons' of the war. To admit
that there was nothing to be learnt from the war would be to founder in
absurdity. The entire veterans' way of thinking rose up against such an
approach.

The stereotype of the veterans' spirit fulfilled a third function that was fundamental to these societies: it was the basis for their existence and proved their unity. This function was particularly important because in reality the societies were numerous and divided. Their unity was scarcely apparent – indeed recruitment was too politically and socially heterogeneous to aid cohesion. To postulate a fundamental unity, sharing the same spirit, made it possible to banish the spectre of division or collapse.

The fourth function of the veterans' spirit was equally important. It allowed officials to specify principles to which all could subscribe. To proclaim, as did Pichot, that the veterans had invented nothing, appeared risky: if they had nothing particular to say, why were they talking? On the contrary – the veterans' spirit and the lessons of the war allowed them to present themselves as the privileged repositories of truths ignored or fudged, even though such truths were part of the common stuff of universal morality.

Thus it is understandable that the existence of the veterans' spirit could not be questioned, even though rhetoric proposed it as highly problematical, describing it as indefinable and speaking of awakening or reanimating it. Without it the societies would have been turned back to their actual divisions. Further, they would have been unable to proclaim any message of national interest; they would have been forced to remain silent. The veterans' spirit was the foundation of both the unity of the generation of fire and its moral authority.

These comments do not allow for any definition of the significance of the veterans' political language. They do however deny any implication of a fascist threat in it.

Part of these arguments is fundamental rhetoric. In order to interpret them it is appropriate to employ a literary type of analysis: their oratorical expansiveness should not be taken as literally as an administrative or judicial report. Further, the veterans stopped short at the level of speech without embarking on action. Certainly they never stopped demanding effective action, but they neither specified nor defined it. Their appeals proliferated, of the type:

> The need remains for us to take action. Our faith in French destinies, our memories of the war, our friendship for the *Poilus*, our faith in the effectiveness of the veterans' movement, our conviction of being able to achieve a little more social justice and peace, all the noble feelings which animate our generous minds – all these are so many reasons to act.
> Action, that is everything.[22]

Or again the phrase 'It's a question of action' from another leader, at the end of an article on the reform of public spirit, a supremely moralising theme:

> Let them rise up, those young men who want to seek the great adventure! It is not a question of mandates or of honours, nor of functions. It is not a question of prolonging the dying agony of a breathless world. It is a question of having a clear eye, a clear mind and a steady heart. It is a question of understanding in order to act, and of acting in order to construct.[23]

Such eloquence has no political action in view.

It is not without significance, on the other hand, that the veterans' rhetoric was aimed at uplifting hearts and developing virtues. In claiming moral authority, the veterans repudiated any immoral behaviour: their morality obliged them to respect right and legality. The only weapons they allowed themselves were those of the just and the wise: persuasion, the influence of devotion and virtue.

At the level of its manner of intervening in politics, the veterans' movement thus appeared entirely contrary to a fascist or fascist-leaning movement. It was impossible for any French fascism to recruit its soldiers of fortune or its strong men from among its respectable and morally high-minded leaders.

Notes to Chapter 5

1. UF 1922 Conference, pp.424–25.

2. Ernest Pezet, speech to the Vichy conference, reproduced in *Combattants et citoyens*, Paris, Spes, 1925, pp.42–43.

3. Ernest Pezet, *La Voix du combattant*, 10 June 1923.

4. Humbert Isaac, 'L'Eveil des consciences', *La Voix du combattant*, 28 October 1923.

5. Camille Héline, *Les Cahiers de l'UF*, 25 March 1939.

6. Appeal displayed in *La Voix du combattant*, 31 March 1934.

7. Léon Viala, *Les Cahiers de l'UF*, 10 January 1937.

8. Aimé Goudaert, *La Voix du combattant*, 9 November 1935.

9. André Gervais, *L'Esprit combattant*, Paris, Ed. de la Revue des vivants, 1927.

10. A. C. no. 7, 645, *Le Cran*, May 1930.

11. *L'Ancien Combattant* (ARAC), May 1919.

12. *Le Combattant sanglier*, May 1930.

13. *La Voix du combattant*, 25 March 1923.

14. *L'Ancien Combattant* (ARAC), July 1919.

15. Speech of the Chairman of the Association des A.C. de Mur-de-Barrez (Aveyron), M. Guitard, to the Assemblée Générale on 10 June 1932, *L'Après-Guerre* (UF, Rodez), October 1932.

16. Marcel Lehmann and Henri Pichot, 'Le role social et l'avenir des associations de Mutilés et Anciens Combattants', *Revue hebdomadaire*, 17 and 24 March 1923, p.491.

17. Louis Boffard, *Le Combattant du Pas-de-Calais*, 10 September 1927.

18. Boffard, *Le Combattant du Pas-de-Calais*, 10 September 1927.

19. Georges Pineau, 'L'esprit combattant', *La Voix du combattant*, 11 November 1927.

20. Report of 23 April 1919, Archives Nationales, F 7/13243.

21. Bonnet, *L'Ame du soldat*, pp.261-2 and p.241. Georges de Tarde's quoted article appeared in *L'Opinion* of 15 January 1917.

22. Georges Pineau, *La Voix du combattant*, 29 April 1923.

23. Dr. Delore, *La Voix du combattant*, 29 July 1933.

6

Veterans' Politics: The Middle Classes and the Régime

The political language of the veterans is too rhetorical, and in particular too moralising, to see any danger of Fascism in it, although this summary conclusion is too negative to be fully satisfactory. What positive interpretation can be derived from these endlessly chewed-over stereotypes of the political party spirit, the veterans' spirit, the general interest's superiority over individual interests, of offering instead of receiving service, etc.? What was the tendency of such arguments and what was their aim?

Denial of Division

The veterans' morality was a denial of division. This is clear in the analysis of difficulties that France was undergoing. The veterans developed the theme of a crisis of morality which relegated economic and social contradictions to the background and almost totally dismissed them. The following article by Humbert Isaac is a typical example:

> Driven by selfishness, activated by money and by an overflowing imagination that distorts the very image of reality, men have once again moved away from the direct path. Nothing healthy or substantial can be achieved without a determined return to Truth, the Law and natural Morality. From the nature of things and the evolution of Civilisation flow inevitable needs to which we must conform for moral Recovery, and the search for a better and more humane order in social, political and economic areas.
>
> What will can guide us through this recovery and this search if not our conscience, our personal conscience, the collective conscience, enlightened by spiritual strength, sustained by moral strength, even tested by suffering? And for whom is an uplifted and tested conscience more necessary than for the Leaders of a group, a nation?
>
> There cannot be any enlightened conscience without an ideal: what ideal

should we reach out to, if not to the brotherhood of man, clinging together in such close solidarity in modern life, then to the brotherhood of Nations leaning increasingly toward such solidarity with Progress. And is it not a work of brotherhood to pursue Justice, the Right to Work, the repression of falsehood and abuse, the suppression of plurality? To achieve a better life for those who suffer hardship, and for their children? To restore the capital to its true social function, to impose on the privileged of the day the sacrifices which we at least have the right to preach?

Note, as in the text of Georges Pineau already quoted, the use of the verb 'to preach' without any pejorative connotation, to designate one of the combatants' contribution to the public debate, and the extreme lack of precision regarding the action under discussion which lies behind the use of military metaphor. Repudiation of political division is entirely explicit in this text written at the end of 1934.

And what principle can be perceived in action, if not 'Unity as at the Front'? We have no wish to believe in the inevitable separation of our fellow citizens of all backgrounds into two camps destined for mutual destruction. We must do everything to persuade rather than to fight, to achieve French unity as the unity of other nations has been achieved – by other means and for other purposes: the will for union to be pursued on all sides, in the Family, at Work, in the Commune, the Region, in the Nation, gradually gathering round a positive doctrine . . . all French people yearning for the ideal.

The structure and the route – surely they are all marked out? Well-ordered freedom – in daily life, in social and working activity, in production and distribution of goods – the State intervening to encourage, to promote where necessary, and to regulate.

Tactics? To go straight ahead, the Veterans in the lead with their banner and the 'Veterans' Spirit', the UNC and the UF if posssible at the forefront, the other groupings following and no doubt the Confederation in its recon-structed form, with 'Youth' in support. Ahead, obstacles, periods of marking time, negotiations, then – forward. We are a mass body. We must awaken and strengthen the Veteran spirit within this body; then successfully con-vince it, give it confidence. Through its demonstrations, to operate in its turn on public Opinion, or, if speed is required, on Public Bodies; assure the maintenance of Peace at home.

To direct this mass we need an élite. Do we not already possess it? Within this élite we must select Leaders; this is the most difficult part . . . it should not be impossible. . . .

The Way of Salvation, not just for a moment but for ever – here, in a few words, is how it appears to whoever considers the search for true Progress:

An objective: the Common Good

A light: the Truth

A guide: Conscience
An ideal: Brotherhood
A principle: Unity
A route: Well-ordered Freedom
A strategy: the Veterans' Spirit in front, with Veterans and Young People
An élite: Advocates, Leaders Along this way, forward, with prudence natural-
ly [sic], but with confidence![1]

This is clearly a text from the right. Despite a few concessions to the left (the right to work, the unity of nations, progress, sacrifices imposed on the privileged), the organic Christian tradition is very strong (family, profession, commune, region). Its morality was shared by the veterans' movement as a whole, however, and similar declarations could be found on the left. Here for example is an article by Henri Pichot, of almost equal date:

> Behind all the distresses of today lies a failing of attitude for . . . all human ills always have a moral cause.
>
> Therein lies the failure of modern capitalism; it is a material and concrete failure because it has been a moral failure. . . . The great leaders of modern capitalism, the industrialists and bankers, scoffed at all moral inspiration and all social obligation: released on to the world like a handmaid of the Apocalypse, science is on a course of self-destruction because it has escaped from the restraints of morality. . . .
>
> What can a *society without a soul* perform for mankind, for the human right to life, for those consumers, each one is a human being, that is to say a living, thinking and feeling soul. . . .
>
> We must restore this world that is wandering and lost.[2]

Morality and Lack of Determination

This moral diagnosis calls for a moral activity of general import: wherever one exists and whatever one does it is always possible to do better or to be better; so is up to each individual to act. The call to action and to the good can thus be addressed to the whole nation without ever defining opponents or allies, without ever specifying a precise action, and in all the texts quoted the total lack of definition of action can be observed. Morality and lack of definition go together: they characterise a discourse where action can do no harm to anyone because it calls each one to be better.

> To veterans who are party members, we say:
> Here is the programme of men who wish 'to Serve'. Examine it. Those who drew it up after thought, research, consultation and agreement, have invented nothing. They admit it.

They have gathered material from right and left. But they claim that on all points of this basic vital programme, agreement is possible, simple. They add: necessary.

If they are right, you will tell them so. You will come to them. It is not the task which is lacking.

You will adopt the ideas in this programme. You will impose them within your parties. You will make them overcome all others.

Go to it with determination. Make plotters reveal themselves, make idealists look at their own feet; share your feelings with the fearful; inject the cautious with your boldness.

Do this, men of the Right, against the egotists who see nothing in Order but a means of preservation. . . . Do this, men of the Left, against the arrivistes who see nothing in the revolution except the means of their own advancement.

By pushing hard, each one of you, you will find yourselves facing each other with your feet on the deflated windbags, the broken idols, the burntout torches, facing each other with your arms ready for the fraternal embrace.

And all France will be with you, the generous and the strong.[3]

This is a text from the right; but the tone on the left is scarcely different:

My dear friends, you must understand the seriousness of the moment.
Your voting paper must carry its full weight in the ballot on May 11. . . .
Prove yourselves men of duty and of thought.

Try to see clearly and plainly. Declarations of affection, even of admiration, and promises will not be in short supply. To make sure of the future, look at the past and do not be dazzled by the mirage of words.

At this hour which is decisive in the realisation of your claims and the march towards your ideals of Justice and Peace, you will no longer be men of party politics, you must endeavour bravely and sincerely to discover which parties will give you the best guarantees for the future.

And when with the power of deliberate conscience you have seen and selected candidates capable of understanding and representing the men of the war, enter the struggle with the energy and serenity gained from the knowledge of a duty to be accomplished.

The time has passed for complaining and useless jeremiads. The time has passed for academic discussion. There is a 'veterans' spirit' to win the day. . . . Caveat consules! – or, let the leaders you have chosen delay no longer with mean activities, and let them watch out! Let them take care not to oppose the faces [sic: in the original, for 'forces'] of movement in the ranks of Veterans.

If it is your wish, my friends, the France of tomorrow will be beautiful. But let your will be guided by deliberation, by awareness, and by memory.[4]

Thus all these trumpeting calls to action, set rhetorically under the emblem of urgency and the necessity (the theme of 'the moment') actually end in a modest invitation to impose the veterans' spirit on all sides. That, in any case, is what was understood by the militants in the ranks, as with these delegates from the Pas-de-Calais:

> It seems much more sensible to me, and in particular more practical, to continue developing the veterans' spirit, to utilise our shared past and the devotion of our militants. Our place is in all social settings, in all the various societies – republican, economic, philanthropic, even electoral committees – to maintain and propagate there the ideas on which we have long agreed. . . .
>
> By bearing our veterans' spirit everywhere without bragging or weakness, we will restore new activity to all failing or misguided organisations and in working to make good the consequences of the terrible past we will reestablish confidence in a better future.[5]

> All our moral activity must, in my view, be directed to remove from the world any ferment of discord and rivalry which could be a future cause for a fresh terrifying cataclysm. And for that, the first condition is that we demand absolute acquiescence in the ideas of humanity, of goodness and of sound mutual understanding that are at the basis of the veterans' spirit, from all those who, on whatever grounds, aspire to take part in the assemblies that direct and govern the nation. . . . Put at our head only elected men imbued with these ideas that emerge from each of our meetings, men who have it in their hearts to work for others, to be without any resentment over unimportant irritations, to dispel selfishness from our relationships.[6]

This morality absolved the veterans from recognising the reality, permanence, and strength of social conflict. They never suggest any representation of society as being divided into antagonistic groups with opposing interests. The very notion of social grouping, still less of social class, is absent from their vocabulary. They treat economic and social factors as specific domains that demand to be organised and represented, integrated into the State. They know the professions. They include societies and among them trade unions, to which they accord much importance. Never, on the other hand, do they analyse a situation or a problem, nor even a crisis, in terms of conflict between social groups with irreconcilable interests.

Nothing reveals this more clearly than the national confederation's unanimously adopted attitude towards the Popular Front. Faced with confrontation between workers and the bourgeoisie, the immediate reaction of the veterans was to invite their goodwill and virtue:

The Veterans . . . distinguish and condemn:

1. The blind conservatism or the indifference of those who might think it possible to maintain certain privileges, to crystallise economic and social evolution in its present state;

2. The recourse to force which nowhere satisfies justice and offers no lasting solution to human problems;

3. Incitements to violence, to hatred, to passion. The Veterans . . . are unanimously agreed in their cry to the Nation, in the grave hours it is now undergoing, that the French people, in dividing themselves, are committing an error and will commit a crime in standing one against another.

They sound the rallying call to all, convinced that France can only be saved through unity, with each person imposing the necessary discipline on himself. They beseech the republicans to understand that the democratic régime will be swept away by one or other of the forms of dictatorship now face to face if the Nation does not through a magnificent effort return to its traditions and rediscover its ancestral virtues.[7]

Conflict between the Generations?

We must not underestimate the political influence of such a stance. The veterans who believed in the existence of a national collectivity higher than the interests of various social groups played an important moderating role here. In addition to workers and employers in close confrontation, the France of the Popular Front consisted of those millions of citizens who repudiated all irremediable division.

Sometimes, it is true, the veterans admitted that society was divided. But for them the true divisions were not economic or social: they were natural. This was the contrast between the older generations, the generation of fire – they used the words 'the men of the war' or 'veterans', with equal meaning – and the coming generation, the young. The generation gap thus formed a substitute for social conflicts and allowed the veterans to accept that the social body was divided, while still refusing to recognise that the divisions were social.

Here, for example, Pichot is facing the breakdown of the Cartel of the left. He headed his article 'This is a dying generation'.

> This is no ordinary ministerial crisis, nor yet a political crisis. It is a social crisis. There is no doubt that this is a dying generation. It is melting, disintegrating; it is in its death throes, it is dissolving . . . already it is decomposing.
>
> Unable to prepare the nation for a war which it did not foresee, it is equally incapable of restoring the nation after victory. For it is into the hands of these people that we have placed the victory.
>
> Do you not recognise these people? They are the same great men who

121

sent you out there in your blue cape and red trousers, with no machine guns and no heavy guns! They are the backroom strategists who thought of shutting you up for three years in barracks instead of arming you against the enemy! And you see in their disbanded cohorts a few of those glorious flag-wavers who threw you into the assault, with your bare bayonets, at fifteen hundred metres!

These are the men whose conceit brazens things out at the moment when public confidence is tottering, when France is sliding towards destitution!
. . .

The world has moved on: they do not perceive it! New ideas are bursting out on all sides: they deny them! Hopes surge up from the heart of the popular and working masses: they take no notice: they are there, that is enough!
. . .

The young people who have managed to slip in among them, how they surround and bind and restrict them. 'Young folk, in too much of a hurry', they say; but in '14, in '15, in '16, in '17, in '18, they did not consider them too young nor in too much of a hurry. How they stood back, to let them pass!

So, silence the chatterers and time-wasters. The people of France are capable of courage. What is money compared with the price of blood? Give us leaders worthy of the name, and worthy of us!

No fake saviour! There was no saviour at the Marne, nor at Verdun. There was the soldier.

Today there is the citizen. He is the same man. Quick march, or take care![8]

This vigorous text, with its noticeably rhetorical and imprecise turn of phrase, made a certain amount of stir,[9] because it expressed a view that was fairly widespread among the veterans, even if it was not the view held by historians. This was confirmed in more moderate terms by Marcel Lehmann:

in the melée of society . . . in which we are swept along, whether we wish it or not, *what are currently in opposition* are not so much political or philosophical systems and formulae as THREE GENERATIONS: the pre-war generation 'which has forgotten nothing and learnt nothing', which, possessing all social powers, clings on desperately; the war generation which has suffered all the consequences of the mistakes of their predecessors but which is rich in a body of experience acquired through hardship and grief; and the post-war generation, too young as yet to have gained experience but greedy for all enjoyment and pleasures, and which is already hurrying to seize everything that offers strength and power.

Our generation is crushed in a vice, caught between the elders who refuse to give up anything – and yet whose time has passed – and the young, who want to push us aside.

Shall we let them get away with it, without having had our turn?
Here lies the true political and social problem of the present moment.[10]

The theme of the three generations reappeared later from time to time, in a somewhat nostalgic fashion:

The generation of the Veterans, caught between the ranks of old men attached to their seat of control and the rising wave of young men, seems to run the danger of disappearing without marking their passage in the history of the post-war era.[11]

Or again:

The generation of fire will have been nothing more than a transitional generation modestly marking a point between the old, which it will have carried on its shoulders for twenty years, and the young who, tomorrow, I must say at once, will seize the reins of the State.[12]

These texts clearly interpreted political malaise as the expression not of social divisions but of rivalry between age-groups, an explanation that may appear surprising. In the veterans' language this analysis was not, however, seen as a somewhat bold interpretation compared to others that were accepted widely and without comment. Its originality was very different: it took political problems seriously, it assumed that they must be explained. In most cases, on the contrary, the ex-soldiers' world saw politics as artificial divisions. Politics did not need to be understood or explained but resisted, and above all despatched elsewhere.

Politics-that-divide

One cannot help being struck by the violence of the veterans' anti-parliamentarianism. It was one of the identifying marks specific to this particular outlook, to the extent that one parliamentary deputy even adopted it for his own use, as if he needed this pass-word to be heard at a veterans' dinner. The scene takes place at the end of the Ardennes UNC conference: an obscure deputy stands and begins his toast:

For a moment I thought I was in the Chamber of Deputies (applause). I, who came here for a bit of a change, who came here to soak myself once more in the spirit of camaraderie, I have been somewhat disturbed.[13]

Even those who were perfectly aware of all that anti-parliamentarianism contained that was hasty and false, even dangerous, did not hesitate to grasp it for their own purposes. There was Henri Pichot, a man of the Left who was nonetheless approved by parliamentarians – the Radical-Socialist Chautemps was to offer him a Deputy's seat in 1935.

In the same text he denounced politicians and the facility with which they were denounced:

> Afflicted by cut-price parties, we are also afflicted by politicians. The politician is a sad creature, and fear nibbles away at him. He is constantly on his guard as if under permanent threat. He sees envy and enemies everywhere. He suspects everything. He sees everything in relation to himself and his own interests. Might not the veterans' movement be a hotbed of replacements?
>
> I do not intend to cast a stone at the man of politics alone. Our public life is contaminated by too many mistaken ideas for him to avoid the charge, even if he prefers to accommodate evil rather than combat it. In this country power, which is only charges and cares, and not even an adequate way of earning one's crust, is supposed to be a source of pleasure and wealth. The French citizen sees his elected representative as an unscrupulous man of ambition, getting his feet under a well-laden table. We keep running down those who direct us, we have dishonoured politics, we make a practice of distrusting government, but we have created a political atmosphere that is infected with jealousy. We have succeeded in the remarkable achievement of turning the deputy into someone of no account, someone rotten, the cause of all ills, and of rendering his function the most coveted and the least worthy of consideration! As soon as someone undertakes any form at all of public life, he finds himself accused of seeking a parliamentary seat.[14]

This is a rare case of clearly argued diagnosis. But why begin by treating the politician as 'a sad creature'?

'No Politics!'

More often the denunciation of politicians avoided the burden of such subtleties. The veterans enjoyed the most pejorative epithets, they delighted in piling up the most derogatory expressions. They were connoisseurs of their respective discoveries. One hesitates to give examples of this assortment, there are so many. Here, first, are a few variations on the theme of old age and the attrition of politicians who have served for a long time: 'Parliamentary old stagers',[15] 'Old campaigners in politics',[16] 'Old political bus-drivers',[17] all appear as bland acknowledgements, like 'old men'.

'Figureheads of advanced age' . . . 'obsolete or distrustful deputies' . . . 'dropped on account of activity'[18] – such phrases designated senators and were sufficient to disqualify them. But the old men who did not take steps to retire lost nothing by waiting:

> Patience, old pictures in moulded frames.[19]

Not to mention such phrases as: 'The old rags of politics, senile for the most part',[20] 'The prostitutes of politics',[21] 'The rejects of the political circus'.[22]

Unremarkable if the politicians were no more than old or tired. But they were treated as corrupt, unworthy and disgusting: these were 'old men, crafty perhaps, but with no aim except their more or less appropriate fame as devious politicians'.[23]

> Politics for them was a trade, and what a trade!
> Politics, the trade of men who can find no other! Politics is a trade which consists of living off the backs of the people without any care for truth or for the public good.[24]

Moreover:

> All these parties with their subtle variations have simply been created by jokers itchy for the presidency, by parliamentarians of course, most of them poor devils like you and me who need to earn their crust and who became politicians just as you become a barman or a waiter, a businessman or a banker, all of them trades without any special qualifications.[25]

So one could present the men of politics as 'professional schemers'[26] and write 'The politicians have turned back to their vomit'.[27]

On the level of vocabulary, this flood of invective offered some interesting inventions, notably words derived from 'la politique' – 'politics' – with pejorative suffixes formed with '-ard' or '-aille'. This offered 'politicard', (politeers) which rhymed with 'combinards' (racketeers) and 'pillards' (thieves)[28] and with 'politique de comitards' (committee politics):[29]

> Politicians – or rather men of committee politics – have for years and years, for their personal profit, applied themselves to setting Frenchmen at each other's throats.[30]

The '-aille' suffix gave 'politicaille', 'politicailler', and 'politicaillon', with implications of 'rabble' or 'rubbish':

> To have doubts about the political rabble that has been bleeding [France] since the Armistice, yes indeed!
> The wings of our idealism have been broken by the wind of internal discord. We have fallen back broken into the muddle, incoherence, swindling, IN A WORD, INTO THE POLITICAILLE.[31]

> If there still remains any one [of the comrades] in whom the spirit of partisan struggles still dominates the veteran spirit, well I will allow myself to tell him frankly and coldly: 'Go away. You are nothing but a false friend and we have no need now of mangy sheep. Go and satisfy your politicking obsession, you will gravitate around our famous politicians of whom many,

too many alas, who claim to be the worthy representatives of the people and who are nothing but common swindlers subject to the pull of money, have stolen from public funds'.[32]

Or again:

> Obscure dabblers in local politics pushed into power by shady schemers.[33]

The tone is clear: it is fairly close to the theme of the clean sweep. It forms the logical conclusion of these imprecations:

> Now comes the time for a settling of accounts for the ineffable outfit in the Palais-Bourbon. Times move on. The timocratic Republic of starvers, shell-manufacturers, shirkers, satraps, time-expired men and 'comrades' is falling into deliquescence and is going to die. At the thought that the mass of ex-soldiers will finally be able to express their wishes freely, a weight is lifted suddenly from our shoulders and great joy seizes the heart at the splendid clean sweep that is in preparation. . . .
>
> And then what does it matter after all, the childishness, the flattery of the mob unleashed on the constituencies? It is a fact well established in the minds of our comrades: with a few exceptions, our legislators have revealed themselves, with cynical ostentation, incapable of extracting the nation from the fuss where their cowardice and stupidity has plunged it.[34]

In this context – and we have taken care to quote exclusively from the UF or UNC newspapers, avoiding any too-easy borrowings from the organs of the extreme right – rejection of politics became an essential element. Politics was dirty, it was disgusting:

> Veterans are fed up with politics, they want no more of it.[35]

> Nothing disgusts us more than politics.[36]

So politics should be avoided. The oft-repeated precept was uncompromising: No Politics.[37]

Partisan Spirit

In almost mythological manner the veterans' discourse thus placed in opposition the worlds of the politician and of the veteran. On one side all the virtues, on the other nothing but vices, and the worst at that. The antithesis between the spirit of party and the veterans' spirit is the Manichean opposition of Good and Evil, the sun and the shadows. A caricature depicts it naively, showing a disabled man leaning on his crutches, soberly dressed with cap and jacket, and a plump pot-bellied man with bowler hat and frock coat. The dialogue is stark:

'To make war you do not need the same qualities as for politics' – 'Oh, that's right, in the latter case, all you need are defects'.[38]

And yet, why this condemnation without mercy? Because the essence of politics is to divide, and to divide Frenchmen artificially. Here too there are innumerable texts. The evocation of political parties almost automatically includes their 'struggles' and their 'disputes':

> The imbecilic battle between the parties.[39]

> The vain and irritating disputes of party and faction.[40]

Moreover, nothing displays the harmful character of politics better than the effects provoked by its irruption into the veterans' world; it was:

> The dirty politics that divide us, at the cost of seeing the men who have done their duty from 1914 to 1918 rail against each other for the greater benefit of the profiteers of our disunity.[41]

This is a persistent theme. It appears naturally on the right:

> Those who attempt to divide us – we know them: it is they who would like to use us for their ambitions and their party hatred. These are the politicians for whom the return to peace was nothing more than a return to the pre-war discords which nearly ruined France and which undoubtedly will destroy her if they begin again. They have learnt nothing, and forgotten nothing.[42]

Or again:

> The Veteran . . . has observed and bitterly deplores the fact that even in our veterans' societies the partisan spirit is still much too strong, that the dirty game of politics still remains by far too much our greatest common divider, and that the veterans' spirit, the national spirit, above party quarrels and questions of individuals or trade is still not, alas, our common denominator. . . . We have no wish . . . to play the game of unscrupulous politicians who are set on dividing the veterans.[43]

It is much more surprising, on the other hand, to meet this same theme developed on the left of the veterans' movement, and even on the extreme left, in the communist ARAC for example. This society made the following appeal:

> ARAC denounces the odious manoeuvres of those broken politicians who have adopted the title of veteran to divide veterans and to trample our sacred rights under foot.[44]

Sometimes it even denied the left/right split, and accused politicians of wanting 'to set the veterans against each other, those of the "left" against those of the "right", thus weakening their capacity for action'.[45]

So powerful was this theme that it sometimes even gave birth to a sort of mythological account of its origins:

> Immediately after the war, all those who live on the quarrels between parties – ruinous for the nation – believed that they were going to be chased out of office; they were at your feet. But you were weary after so many struggles; you were too happy to be back home again where the accumulation of work absorbed your activity. And the politician took hope: he manoeuvred us, multiplying veterans' societies to oppose one against another and to neutralise their activity.[46]

The same conviction animated the obscure author of the moral balance-sheet presented to the general assembly of the *Poilus de Sainte-Sigolène* (Haute-Loire) in 1931:

> At the time of demobilisation the *Poilus* were seen as demigods, and if they had sought it, all the low-grade politicians would have been swept away by them in elections.
>
> Having won the war and saved France, they would have assured the peace and led the Nation.
>
> But after the long and terrible psychological and physical shock imposed on them by the war the veterans needed a time of rest.
>
> This rest time was used by the politicians. Their motto was 'Divide and Rule'. In some cases they formed *Poilu* societies themselves, but with the aim of opposing one against another.
>
> The result: an untidy cluster of groups, disunity, conflict of interests, impotence and even discredit.[47]

Such, in broad terms, was the veterans' stereotype speech on politics. Its rhetoric and moralising style did not wholly remove all sparkle: beyond the evocation of the veterans' spirit as the reincarnation of all traditional civic virtues contrasting with condemnation of the politicians' party spirit, it obstinately refused to see society as being fundamentally divided. There was no finality in the split: either it could be explained by inter-generational conflicts which must be accommodated as a fact of life, or it emanated from party politics and was totally artificial.

The Significance of Veteran Stereotypes

This insistence on denying social conflict and denouncing politics as the sole cause of division among French people was too generalised, too constant, to escape notice. Three factors appear to be responsible.

The first does not require lengthy explanation. It was limited to noting that the veterans' discourse was not entirely mistaken, rather that it lacked balance. It was wrong less in what it said than in what it did not say. The accent stressed too heavily what French people have in common with each other, obliterating points of divergence. But it is not untrue that all French people do indeed have much in common: language, culture, history, interests. It is difficult, between two world wars, to see nation-wide elements as artificial or secondary. Given the experience on which their groups were founded, the veterans' particular sensitivity to points of solidarity is easily understood; that in return they were blind to social conflict is surprising: why deny such a body of evidence?

Social Marginality

At this juncture we should no doubt consider the position of the veterans' movement in society, for in fact it was not a precise reflection of the nation. Although there were industrial workers in this mass organisation, they were under-represented, while farmers, shop assistants and tradesmen were over-represented. It was a movement of the provincial lower and middle bourgeoisie, recruiting its leaders from teachers in primary and secondary schools, minor civil servants and middle managers, tradesmen and travelling salesmen as well as lawyers and doctors. There were few industrialists among them, few of the higher ranks of the private sector, few very wealthy men, very few of the provincial notability solidly rooted in the old bourgeoisie of property-owning landlords. Popular but not proletarian in its recruitment, the veterans' movement was managed by the middle classes. Dominant in its leadership were the reservist non-commissioned officers, former senior primary school pupils who through merit and hard work had achieved solid comfort and respectability without the connections of grander families. They were semi-notable, insufficiently rich, educated, well-known, or influential to share power with the true notables. Those already established pushed them away when they did not need them. The national press, in the hands of businessmen, took an interest in them as long as they appeared useful. In the social system the veterans were thus marginal; they did not attain power, even indirectly through the pressure-group to which they belonged.

Marginal, and keenly aware of their marginality, the veterans' association leaders – unlike the workers – could not accept their situation as a relationship of exploitation and domination to be overturned through revolutionary action or openly contested, as in a strike. The proletariat had even less access to power than the middle classes but used its exclusion as a starting point for attempts to reverse the situation. Acknowledging its own exclusion, it aimed to acquire power to exclude in turn those who were currently dominant.

The middle classes were too taken up with social advancement and conquest of the notability to adopt a proud stance outside society as it existed, to announce their exclusion and attempt to dominate it. They had no opening except to deny, as a matter of principle, the exclusion of which they were the victims, and to assert very firmly the universal values of democracy and national unity. To emphasise the union of all French people was, for those who felt excluded from power, a way of reclaiming their centrality and participation in that power. In reversing officially-proclaimed democratic principles and turning them against the ruling classes the veterans sought to play a role which was denied them; in fact, if the democratic ideal of the general interest were taken seriously, the middle classes in their median position would become the arbiters of conflicting interests. Their numbers are sufficiently great and the ideology of the general interest, taken seriously, would require the highest consideration of their views.

After all, it is entirely logical that the middle classes should refuse to analyse society as a hierarchical and conflictual ensemble of groups or classes. Firstly, they are much too heterogeneous, divided by multiple contradictions: the interests of farmers and consumers are directly opposed on matters of agricultural prices. The public sector and the security it offers are in opposition to the private sector: they represent two different ways of seeking social promotion, through the civil servants' diploma or through the initiative and risk of the craftsman or trader. Secondly, the middle classes have no common meeting ground in the great conflict between workers and the bourgeoisie. They do not identify with either group, and cannot truly choose one side without betraying themselves. Their members are attracted socially upwards, and their individual desire for promotion lies in their aspiration to join the bourgeoisie. But they calculate all that separates them from it, and they are sensitive to the fact that the bourgeoisie is closed to them; its exclusiveness they interpret in moral terms, as a form of selfishness and not as a natural reaction of preservation of privileges. Thus they cannot ally themselves wholly with this social environment which does not admit them. Further, they are still too close to the popular classes to repudiate their origins, and yet they distance themselves from them. It is therefore particularly difficult for them to find a precise place in a society dominated by the conflict between the working classes and the bourgeoisie.

To overcome this problem and avoid a difficult choice the middle classes naturally tend to reject the very notion of social class. This allows them both to retain their relative superiority and at the same time to hide their enduring, though reduced, inferiority. It is therefore logical that there is no organisation of the middle classes as such, but that they attach themselves to civic organisations apparently unrelated to social divisions, which in fact enable them to express themselves and to affect decisions: the veterans' societies and those of taxpayers or consumers are perfectly suited to this role. The denial of a class structure is the surest way to avert any representation of a society divided into classes. But since the need for structure remains, the structure of the middle classes adopts the appearance of a purely civic system. The link between the rationale of the veterans' movement and the social adherence of its spokesmen then becomes more comprehensible. Through the mediation of the veterans' spirit and the general interest – which are not purely pretexts, as we have shown – it was indeed the voices of clerks, teachers at different levels, travelling salesmen, traders, bank employees and farmers who are talking.

Political Marginality

This social analysis is inadequate. It takes account of the psychological rationale and the appeal to great principles, as well as of the blindness to social conflicts – or calls for unity when it was no longer possible to blind oneself – for instance at the time of the Popular Front. It does not explain the vehemence of anti-parliamentarianism.

The marginality of the veterans' movement within the political system should be noted here. In this short book it is not possible to expose all their ideas in detail, nor to describe their activity as a disinterested pressure group. Their dossiers on international relationships, the politics of health, etc., were substantial; but they never succeeded in influencing political decisions. Effective when pursuing a material claim, the pressure of the ex-soldiers had no impact when tackling questions of general interest. Everything happened as if the leadership – but also, at a wider level, public opinion – was restricting them to their material claims, distancing them more effectively from general preoccupations. When they demanded money, they were given money, but this was in part to silence them, and to gain the right to ignore them if they meddled in international debt, the organisation of the League of Nations, or governmental reform. The ruling classes were in any case entirely igno-

rant of the veterans' general or civic activity. The only article that the
solemn and serious *Revue politique et parlementaire* devoted to the veterans was a tissue of idiocy,[48] and they could find no politician in favour
of governmental reform quoting veterans' works on the topic even when
he could have claimed their support.

This deafness of the professionals to amateurs is more intolerable
because they, the professionals, offered manifold evidence of their inadequacy. The veterans included very competent leaders in their ranks,
who proved their managerial ability in founding and developing their
societies and charitable work, achievements that should certainly have
earned them an audience: but even while it foundered in impotence, the
political system denied them any right to speak. Such politicans provided multifarious verbal concessions as they concluded their after-dinner
speeches with fine flourishes, but in practice they refused them all access
to power. The veterans talked to thin air, Cassandra figures whose fore-
sight did not dissuade politicians from precipitating the loss of the
nation.

Republican Dissatisfaction

It must be admitted, in fact, that the parliamentary system was not
working perfectly in France at this time. Before imputing the veterans'
virulent anti-parliamentarianism to some sort of authoritarian or reac-
tionary nostalgia, it should be conceded that it was not entirely without
foundation. The collapse of the Third Republic in 1940 and the Fourth
in 1958 were too close to the prophecies of disaster held by the veterans
to reproach them summarily for their anti-parliamentarianism.

It is very striking that the veterans' anti-parliamentarianism was not
restricted to the right-leaning UNC but also represented the republican
teachers of the UF and the radicals of the FNCR. The criticism of
Pichot, for example, when it broke away from its usual rhetoric, was not
without force. In a report that caused a sensation, following the
February 6th riots, he sought the restoration of governmental authority:

> We must *recreate the political instrument of power.* Any reform of French
> life first requires reconstitution of the *political instrument* that a genuine gov-
> ernment provides.
>
> It is in vain that so many programmes are currently launching themselves
> into political meetings, the press, reviews, discussions. No party can hope to
> fulfil its programme because the *political instrument* to achieve it does not
> exist.
>
> Current struggles are meaningless as long as power is not restored.
> Dissolution of the Chamber now would achieve nothing. The parties would

struggle in electoral battle for possession of a shadow of power, a shadow of government.[49]

This feeling of a state falling apart, this irritation in the face of ministerial instability, can be found in every issue of the *Poilu républicain*, the organ of the FNCR. This, it may be recalled, was a society founded by a notorious freemason on the eve of the 1924 elections to combat the influence of the UNC. The officials of the FNCR came from radical and socialist milieux, and they therefore found the evolution of the régime disturbing.

Is it not heartbreaking to observe that the men who direct the destiny of a nation do not, when they are in power, carry out the programmes elaborated within their respective parties? The effect of governmental majorities obliges them to make such concessions to the groups of their majority or their support that all bold initiatives and genuine collaboration are eliminated.

To this should be added the ever-growing appetites of those who also wish to taste power, and we understand better how governments pass away or succeed each other without any apparent improvement in the crises we suffer, to the great dismay of popular common sense. . . .

From there to accusing the régime of being rotten and exhausted from top to bottom is only a small step. All the societies, and all the parties who might gain from vilifying the republican régime, have therefore promptly done so, and that is why we see today so many attacks on parliamentary rule, on the impotence of the State, on the régime.

Should this wave of pessimism discourage all who are firmly attached to the principles and the institutions of this Republic and who wish to see it more solid, more just, and more humane?

If our conscience and our reason oblige us to condemn partisan politics that sacrifice the general interest and the future of the nation to the satisfaction of private and selfish interests, we should in the meantime find within ourselves the strength and energy necessary to impose effective power on the nation, without weakness, the vigilant protector of the law and the fundamental institutions of the Third Republic. . . .

The reform of the Constitution is becoming a necessity if we wish to achieve harmony among all the nation's active powers. If it does not appear necessary in the eyes of certain political parties, it can however only be envisaged when a republican majority comes to power. To procrastinate in the face of difficulties that may await the advocates of this reform is perhaps more dangerous, for we do not know what tomorrow holds in store for us.

It behoves the ex-soldiers of the FNCR to show that their devotion to the Republic is a function of the national organisation.[50]

These lines were written before 6 February 1934, an occasion which may be perceived as likely to strengthen the movement in favour of the reform of governmental institutions. For confirmation of this it is necessary only to read the first editorial of Fonteny, the chairman-founder of the FNCR, immediately following that date:

> Public opinion is stirred. Tomorrow it will be distressed. However, nothing is being done to remedy it. More, nothing can be done with the current functioning of our institutions.
>
> Statesmen have visited Russia and have praised the results of the five-year-plan system.
>
> Parliamentary deputies have visited Italy and were surprised by the transformation of that nation since the arrival of Fascism. But Mussolini has been governing Italy for ten years, and the Soviet régime has been installed in Russia for more than fifteen years.
>
> In France we have had twenty-seven ministers since the war, some of whom lasted for two years, at the most, and others four days.
>
> How can a government make long-term plans for reform if it cannot be certain that it will still be in power in a week's time?
>
> Was not the 1933 budget put forward by the ministers Herriot, Paul-Boncour and Daladier successively, and that of 1934 by the Daladier, Sarraut and Doumergue governments?
>
> In his memoirs General André* writes: 'The Government spends three-quarters of its time defending its existence, it has only one quarter left to attend to national affairs'.

The perpetuation of this state of affairs put the régime in danger.

> Modifications must be introduced with all speed. How? Within the framework of our institutions. By what means?
>
> The question is put to the FNCR, it must respond, but already our 11th national conference has decided to pursue the study of constitutional reform through the strengthening of popular authority and control, the introduction of effective governmental responsibility, economic and social representation, administrative and judicial reform, and the adaptation of parliamentary modes of work.
>
> It is to this indispensable task that, from this very day, all republicans should devote themselves.[51]

The strong feeling of dissatisfaction over the functioning of parliamentary institutions was not, as can be seen, the attribute of the right lamely and tardily rallying to the Republic. The heirs of radical and

---

*General André had been the Minister of War of the most anticlerical Republican Government before the First World War, that of the Radical-socialist Combes. He had been compelled to resign for having inquired after the personal religious views of the officers he had to promote. Only a left-wing Republican could quote General André, who was totally rejected by the right.

socialist tradition shared it. It was not, on the other hand, a purely negative reflex of hostility; beyond the ordinary rhetorical end-of-confer-
ence common ground it led to reflection that was both serious and
moderate. The combination of governmental reform projects proposed
by ex-soldiers' associations, the UF, the UNC, or the FNCR, were in
effect a reasonable response to the functional defects of the régime. This
will be touched on in conclusion. We are very far from the authoritarian solutions of fascist or Hitlerian inspiration; the cliché antiparliamen-
tarianism of the veterans did not foster encouragement for a coup d'état
or dictatorship, but for a proposed modern republic. We cannot conclude better on this point than with the words of one of the great leaders of the veterans' movement, a former chairman of the UF and tireless
activist of the whole inter-war period, René Cassin, who wrote in a sort
of balance-sheet, after emphasising fully the positive support from the
veterans' clubs:

> The true setback . . . is that the Third Republic, weakened by the colossal
> losses suffered in 1914–1918 and by the sacrifices demanded of all, was not
> politically and socially reformed before the testing moments of international
> life.[52]

Notes to Chapter 6

1. Humbert Isaac, 'La Voie du Salut', *La Voix du Combattant*, 29 December 1934.

2. Henri Pichot, *Les Cahiers de l'UF*, 15 March 1934.

3. Pierre Franchard, *La Voix du Combattant*, 2 February 1935.

4. Paul Patou, *Le Combattant du Pas-de-Calais*, 1 April 1924.

5. C. Montreuille, *Le Combattant du Pas-de-Calais*, November 1926.

6. Fleury Cresson, *Le Combattant du Pas-de-Calais*, 10 August 1928.

7. *Journal des mutilés*, 6 December 1936. This appeal was extracted and distributed as a separate pamphlet by the Confederation.

8. *Journal des mutilés*, 18 November 1925.

9. This article was reproduced in provincial newspapers, notably in *Le Combattant du Pas-de-Calais*, January 1926.

10. Marcel Lehmann, 'L'Etau', *Journal des mutilés*, 9 January 1926.

11. Victor Beauregard, *La Voix du Combattant*, 5 May 1928.

12. Henri Pichot, *Les Cahiers de l'UF*, 15 April 1935.

13. *Le Combattant sanglier*, April 1933.

14. Henri Pichot, 'Partis et politiciens', *Journal des mutilés*, 16 June 1923.

15. Georges Pineau, *Le Poilu du Centre*, December 1933.

16. Paul Patou, *Le Combattant du Pas-de-Calais*, 5 January 1924.

17. Paul Vaillant, *La France mutilée*, 16 March 1924.

18. Paul Galland, *La Voix du combattant*, 1 January 1927.

19. Hubert-Aubert, *La Voix du combattant*, 12 December 1925.

20. J. Vèze, *Le Poilu du Centre*, May 1925.

21. See note 16.

22. Gaston Vidal, then acting chairman of the UF, in the UF's first national weekly, *Après la bataille*, 9 November 1919.

23. Victor Beauregard, *La Voix du combattant*, 5 September 1925.

24. Abbé Bernard Secret, *La France mutilée*, quoted in *Le Poilu du Centre*, January 1924.

25. Adet, *Après le combat* (UF, Marseille), July 1935.

26. See note 18.

27. Hubert-Aubert, *La Voix du combattant*, 15 October 1938.

28. Laurent Coupiac, *L'Après-Guerre*, July 1934.

29. Léon Viala, *Les Cahiers de l'UF*, 10 October 1938.

30. Hubert-Aubert, *La Voix du combattant*, 16 Janaury 1937.

31. André Wilhelm, *L'Ancien Combattant* (UF, Nancy), 15 February 1926.

32. Mourton, *Le Poilu de Centre*, March 1934.

33. See note 16.

34. *La Tribune de Nice* (UF), 25 September 1919.

35. See note 24.

36. Henri Pichot, *Journal des mutilés*, 16 October 1938.

37. References would be beyond numbering, so frequently recurrent was this formula in the veterans' press..

38. *Le Poilu de la Loire* (Semaine du combattant), March 1931.

39. Henri Pichot, *Les Cahiers de l'UF*, 1–15 August 1934.

40. Pichot, *Les Cahiers de L'UF*, 15 November 1934.

41. See note 20.

42. Commandant Du Plessis, *Le Poilu d'Anjou et du Maine* (UNC), July 1921.

43. A. Loez, *Le Combattant des Deux-Sèvres* (UNC) September 1934.

44. *Le Réveil des combattants* (ARAC), 11 April-10 May 1935.

45. *Le Réveil des combattants* (ARAC), 11 February-10 March 1936.

46. Emile Taudières, *La Voix du combattant*, 23 May 1925.

47. *Le Poilu de la Loire*, February 1931.

48. *Revue politique et parlementaire*, 10 July 1934, unsigned article.

49. Henri Pichot, report to the federal council of the UF dated 11 March 1934, *Les Cahiers de l'UF*, 15 March 1934.

50. J. Panhaleux, 'Révisons la constitution', *Le Poilu républicain*, December 1933.

51. A-J. Fonteny, 'Et maintenant?', *Le Poilu républicain*, February 1934.

52. Personal letter from René Cassin to the author.

7

Preface to Vichy and the Fourth Republic

Although the veterans' movement had its roots in the vivid and painful past of the war, and although the origins of its anti-militarism and its pacifism – with all its heavy consequences – lay there, its political language and stereotyped morality offer in contrast glimpses of subsequent development.

The veterans' movement did not prefigure some form of French fascism. On the contrary, by assembling the middle classes in respect for republican morality and legality, it constituted a powerful obstacle to the development of true fascism in the France of the 1930s. Refusing to specify political adversaries, let alone their violent elimination, the movement resisted the leagues' activist style and took its stance in a moral guidance without direct influence on political life. It was the exact opposite of an organisation created to take power.

On the other hand, they should take power, as if miraculously, respecting legality, without violence and without internal French divisions; this power should have as its aim the reign of morality in public life; it should preach the sacrifice of individual interests for the general interest, necessary discipline and traditional virtues – undoubtedly the above scenario would answer the wishes of the veterans, and this they would uphold.

The Vichy View

This is exactly what happened under the Vichy government, particularly because the man in power, both moralist and strong, was the very incarnation of the veterans' spirit, of Verdun and of victory. The veterans would not have supported a man of factional leanings in taking over the government. Once Pétain was in place with the agreement of

Notes to this Preface can be found on page 147.

Parliament and the unanimous support of the people, his régime and his discourse responded to veterans' expectations. He could remove elected mayors and imprison politicians: these were individual measures taken legally and the veterans never ceased to claim that justice must be enforced against dishonest or incompetent individuals.

It went further. Pétain was not content to take up the veterans' moral theme: he adopted the same causes. Here finally was a régime that was not concerned with politics but took an interest in real problems – or at least those identified as such by the veterans: health, hygiene, the birth-rate. He preached French cohesion and rejected considerations of social class, he spoke of professions where others saw workers and employers challenging each other. Although some veterans hesitated to recognise themselves in a government that placed Jews, even those who had fought in the war, in a special category, that proscribed popular consultation and took increasingly military forms, most were fully won over, or at least satisfied. The destination of veterans' discourse was neither Hitler nor Mussolini; it was Pétain.

A major text illustrates this convergence: the manifesto solemnly adopted by the UNC at their meeting in the Salle Wagram in October 1933. It deserves a lengthy quotation because as well as announcing the Pétainist approach it refers, as if casually, to most of the themes we have been analysing; it includes a moral interpretation of the economic crisis, a rightist reference to the consequences of the French Revolution, and, under 'Directives for Action', an appeal to morality, spirituality and selflessness:

> In the face of global instability and growing problems, the time has come for decision and for action.
>
> The *UNION NATIONALE DES COMBATTANTS*, obedient to its conference resolutions, has a duty to denounce the causes of evil and to seek remedies for them.
>
> Setting itself above party politics and within the strict framework of public benefit, the Union sees it as its duty to define the spirit, the moral atmosphere and the major direction of the movement of RECOVERY and RENEWAL that is imperative.
>
> Findings
>
> The business crisis persists and unemployment affects too many workers of all kinds.
>
> As a result of the worldwide imbalance between Production and Consumption, men without work fall into destitution and are swept towards revolution and war.
>
> Through the habit of easy gains acquired during the war, through manip-

ulations of contracts, through monetary crisis and speculation, through excessive credit, principles of work, saving and integrity have been seriously undermined. The excessive disparity between costs to Producers and prices to Consumers is severely affecting both producer and consumer.

Honesty and confidence are vanishing from social relationships: selfishness and materialism are triumphant.

Young people, even more than we ourselves, are worried about the future.

By suppressing collective interests in the form of corporations, the revolution of 1789 left the State and the Individual confronting each other.

In modern times we find citizens claiming once again the right to unite in defence of their interests. The official establishment has not yet adjusted to this change. Unions and professional associations clash and cripple the State, which lacks the necessary authority to decide between them and to overrule them.

Partisan activity and demagoguery aggravate such conflicts. This is anarchy.

The old solutions have failed.

Faced with potentially converging internal and external dangers, anxiety increases and doubt overwhelms even our leaders.

If the appropriate reforms do not bring about the necessary developments, revolution will impose them through force.

Directives for Action

The time has passed for temporary expedients and compartmentalised solutions. We must have the courage to be ambitious and to prepare for a new order.

The fundamental origin of the evil lies in men's minds. The primary reform is that of public attitudes.

We must:

Serve, instead of seeking self-service. Fulfill duties before claiming rights. Set moral and spiritual values above material values. Turn against dishonesty, demoralisation and selfishness. Combat sectarianism in all its forms and no matter what its source. Rediscover the worth of home and family. Restore human dignity.

Have the courage to demand the prompt suppression of abuses, sinecures and plurality of office.

Strike without mercy against corruption no matter where it occurs, however high-placed the guilty.

Reestablish the social order on its two natural foundations: Family and Profession.

The State has been compelled to concern itself with everything, and even those who have sought its intervention have later had to free themselves from its grip.

The concept of the pastoral state tends to replace individual effort.

We must:

– Restore authority, provide it with sufficient stability, free it from the intolerable tyranny of parties and factions, of greed and the power of money.

– Ensure the strict separation of powers and the independence of the magistrature.

– Undertake financial recovery. Seek budgetary stability through immediate cutting of all unnecessary expenditure and the energetic repression of fraud and waste.

– Avoid excessive taxes and inflation, the creators of destitution and ruin.

– Simplify public accounting and suppress useless and costly bureaucratic paperwork.

– Prepare the administrative reorganisation that will reduce burdens on the State and thereby make fiscal reform possible.

This will ensure a higher return from taxes with less burdensome rates, which will effectively bring about a reduction in the cost of living.

The will to restrict and confine the State, which inspired this long excursus, is striking. It is indeed the ideology of the middle classes of the private sector: it is far removed from the exaltation of the all-powerful State that was characteristic of fascist regimes. To continue:

How can RECONSTRUCTION be envisaged, except on the following lines:

In social areas:

– The Individual, respected as such, who should advance harmoniously in intellectual, moral and physical domains;

– Full of a sense of family and of society;

– Sustained in his physical and moral well-being, in his culture; protected in his home, his work, his leisure;

– Encouraged to work, to save, to achieve ownership;

– Social relationships based on good faith, justice, BROTHERHOOD;

– Social activities of all kinds, even intellectual, organised in associations, activities of a professional nature in unions; all grouped by category, and together, regionally or nationally, so as to achieve a better understanding and harmonisation of their needs and better results, for their own benefit and that of the whole nation. Through their integration in the nation's life, the State will become not only a political but also a SOCIAL entity.

In Economic areas:

– A Régime preserved from capitalist excesses, demagogic illusions and state tyranny.

– WORK, manual or intellectual, honoured – work on the land first of all – protected, justly shared to avoid unemployment and demoralising allowances as far as possible; progressive improvement of conditions, with mothers remaining at home.

– Encouragement and protection for saving; speculation discouraged and heavily taxed; avoidance of exaggerated concentration of capital or credit, national or international.

– The defeat of idleness, hoarding, the selfish and stupid use of money.

– CAPITAL obliged to submit its driving principle of profit to the principle of social function to be fulfilled; devoted to the service of economic and social activities; freed from the excessive weight of certain of the charges and risks that it bears today; leaving more of the results of production to Labour and to its reserve institutions.

With the average conditions of the majority thus improved, Labour and Capital will be more closely interdependent.

– Production in the service of the common good, within controlled freedom, directed towards quality, protected from excessive risks by the development of the union organisation itself; with smaller amounts paid in taxes, leading to reduced prices for the consumer and for export to the colonies and foreign markets.

– The Distribution of products also managed in a professional manner, with only truly necessary intermediaries.

– The State intervening only as a last resort to arbitrate in persistent conflicts.

––––––––––

To assure the FRENCH PEACE, we must:

– Strengthen FRENCH UNITY, at home and in the colonies.

– Severely chastise anti-national activities.

– In foreign policy, combine concern for international solidarity with concern for SECURITY. Genuinely seek agreement with other nations, whatever their internal régime. Remain strong and vigilant in the face of multiple exterior threats.

Call to the Nations

– DUTIES acknowledged and respected in the light of the Common Good;

– INFLATION avoided and finances strengthened;

– FRENCH UNITY reinforced;

– NATIONAL SECURITY guaranteed;

– INTERNATIONAL UNDERSTANDING sought;

– BROTHERLY COLLABORATION between French people, at home and in the colonies;

– WORK assured for all;

– The SOCIAL STATE finally constructed.

THIS IS WHAT WE WANT!

THIS is what our beliefs, our experience of life and of the war gives us the right to propose as the basis for the New Order.

VETERANS, conscious of the strength represented by 865,000 comrades united as at the front in the ranks of the U.N.C.,

Ardent YOUTH, with life and strength before you,
LEADERS concerned for the future,
FRENCH PEOPLE of all conditions, but strong in purpose,
Join us in our efforts.
At work, let us all dispel scepticism to return to Faith in our Nation
which led us to Victory,
let us rise energetically to the measure of the times.
Remember that historic Destiny is often created from national renunciation.
Once again, let us be worthy of our Nation and of Humanity.[1]

Public Safety

This text's leanings to the right are obvious, and it foreshadows Vichy in more than its morality: the denial of revolutionary individualism, the insistence on natural groupings and distrust of the State here clearly show loyalty to conservative traditions. But republican tradition leads equally to approval of the full powers confided to Marshal Pétain in the name of the jacobin demands of public welfare. It is necessary simply to listen to Pichot's opening speech at the 1938 UF conference, addressed to ten thousand veterans on the promenade des Anglais in Nice (extracts):

What the French have done they can do again: they need only to will it and to follow the enduring laws which create strong nations. We are a free people; but the victory over ourselves, over ephemeral surrenders and too easy mistakes, will come from our productive submission to the spirit of public safety:

– Public safety! No liberty without order and without discipline; the preservation of liberty lies in men's moderation and in the nation's wisdom; a nation loses its freedom only when it has not made good use of it;

– Public safety! It is in labour, in continual creation, that the true wealth of men and of nations lies, in the indissoluble alliance of the mind that conceives and calculates and the hand that executes; without this there is no hope, for there is no benefit in labour if there is no conscience in labour.

– Public safety! Public safety! Nothing is born, preserved or passed on except through citizens' unity, in civic harmony and social brotherhood. Woe be to nations who tear themselves apart; they are prey for States without conscience! French people, you who say that danger will revive the Union, I must tell you that the union must be created ahead of the danger, for it is the union that will prevent the danger!

Love of freedom, respect for good order, conscience in labour, concern for justice and a feeling of national brotherhood, these are the indestructible pillars of a united France.

Soldiers and fellow citizens, we are not afraid to proclaim our duty to the world. Only the major nations live in enlightenment and eventually possess the truth; Frenchmen that we are, it is up to us, scorning empty words, to prove that democracy draws from itself purer and more durable values than the rough and simplistic command of any single entity, whether a man, a party or a class – because democracy, under pain of self-betrayal and self-delusion, believes in man's rationality, protects his dignity and rests on the culture of the spiritual values that ennoble life and raise man above himself.[2]

Constitutional Reforms

For the veterans, however, Vichy offered an exceptional cure for an exceptional situation. The régime in essence matched their aspirations, but it was not exactly what they had been hoping for. The Vichy tone, its moralising and rallying attitudes, its social preoccupations, accorded well with the veteran spirit, but on the other hand the new institutions of the French state – or rather the absence of true institutions in this régime resting on a single man – wholly failed to meet veterans' expectations.

On matters of constitutional reform, veterans' thinking in fact turned in a very different direction. With few shades of difference the UF and the UNC came to the same conclusions and specified reinforcement of the executive, rationalisation of parliamentary work and expansion of economic and social democracy, but no limiting of freedom, abandonment of parliamentary rule or retreat from universal suffrage. It was a matter of amending the régime, not of overturning it to substitute a different régime based on different principles. Even the boldest veterans, those quickest to specify constitutional reform, did not envisage abandoning the Republic which they never rejected as the rightist nationalists of the Action Française or the Ligues did. Here, for example is the central passage from the final motion of the inter-society conference organised by the *Semaine du combattant* on February 27 and 28, 1932 – i.e., well before the second electoral success of the coalition of the socialist and the radical parties before the period of ministerial instability that brought the theme of constitutional reform to the top of the agenda:

Observing that the nation is suffering from a moral, social, economic and political crisis that is plaguing the whole world and that endangers Peace;

Observing that our constitutional system no longer corresponds to the realities of today and therefore shows itself incapable of effectively resolving current problems;

Resolved to remain within the framework of republican institutions adopted by the nation;

Demand a reform of the Constitution on the following principles:

1. The Executive: should be strong in its powers, limited in its prerogatives, effectively responsible, assured of the stability essential to its continuity of action.

2. The Legislature: should be independent, its methods of operation reorganised, its task simplified, laws of a technical nature being prepared or proposed by competent organisations.

3. Economic and Social issues: those in charge of these areas should acquire representation and participate in the State councils which will employ their abilities while supervising them and establishing their responsibilities.

4. A Supreme Court: should be introduced, charged with assessing conformity of laws with the Constitution so that the liberty of each citizen or each group can be effectively guaranteed.[3]

This document, taking up earlier texts of more restricted circulation, shows that for the veterans there was nothing hasty about constitutional reform. No doubt it appeared particularly pressing immediately after 6 February 1934, but the veterans did not wait for this episode before discussing it. Their reflections showed deep dissatisfaction with the functioning of the parliamentary régime, and the solutions that they specified foreshadowed the Fourth Republic rather than a dictatorship.

Among dozens of texts the general motion of the UF national conference in 1934 offers proof of this assertion:

GENERAL PROGRAMME

A. CONSTITUTIONAL REFORM

1. Constitutional Reforms:

a) The function of *Président du Conseil* to be endowed by statute:

– The *Président du Conseil* should be without portfolio. The Présidence du Conseil to be supported by autonomous services independent of other ministerial services and based in a major national headquarters;

– The *Président du Conseil* to take office, in principle, immediately following parliamentary elections, for the life of the parliament;

– Any ministerial crisis leading to a change in general policy may be followed by dissolution of the Chamber of Deputies, the people as sole sovereign remaining the final arbiters.

b) Economic powers, formally established in Unions and Professional Associations, to obtain representation in each Region and in the Nation by means of a National Economic Council.

Consultation of this Council to be obligatory, with governmental powers to pass regulatory decrees on the advice of this Council.

The National Economic Council to have in addition a mission of concili-ation, arbitration and jurisdiction in economic matters.

c) A Legislative Committee, composed of deputies and lawyers, to be empowered to draw up the final text of laws adopted by Parliament prior to the final debate and vote, so that they may always be accurate, clear, and capable of precise interpretation.

2. Regulatory Measures:

a) Parliamentary procedures to be reformed, in particular those concern-ing powers which Parliamentary Commissions have arrogated to themselves over the years; the right of amendment and the right of initiative on Expenditure to be regulated.

b) In order to clear up parliamentary customs, the following measures are envisaged:

– Validation of elections by the *Conseil d'Etat* and not by the assemblies;

– Regulation of professional incompatibility;

– Members of assemblies to be required to devote all their time to the exercise of their mandate during the sessions;

– Regulation and restriction of the right to vote by proxy;

– Adoption of a system of Proportional Representation with votes for women and a reduction in the number of deputies.

These technical measures were aiming at moralizing parliamentary life. Each Assembly, the Chambers of Deputies as the Senate, had the power to decide if its members had been regularly elected. The validation was thus dependent on majority rule. By giving the validation power to an independent administrative jurisdiction, the proposal had a clear moral purpose. The professional incompatibilities meant forbidding a deputy to continue being a barrister, or a businessman, and more generally, to have occupations which would benefit from the deputy or senator's function. The general motion continues:

B. THE NATION'S ECONOMIC LIFE

1. Principle: Integrated economic liberalism has had its day: as with other forms of freedom, economic liberty should be regulated in the general inter-est.

2. Applications. : . . .

C. MEANS OF ACTION

The campaign in favour of the Federal Union has already contributed substantially to the revival of belief in national solidarity and social and civic discipline, and will persist in its efforts.

It expresses the determination that the will for Reforms, Social Justice and Economic Recovery within democratic institutions which is stirring the hearts of the whole nation can concentrate swiftly on the Veterans' appeal in a short and substantial programme for French renewal.[4]

These serious and carefully considered proposals have a very different ring from the customary anti-parliamentary orations. Organisation of the *Conseil* presidency? – Sarraut and Blum were soon to put this into practice. The separate investiture of the President of the Council would follow, under the Fourth Republic. Dissolution without previous notice to the Senate? This was proposed by the *ad hoc* commission of the Chamber of Deputies in 1934. True, Doumergue was overthrown in November for taking up this idea for himself, but the radicals who thus protected the deputies to some extent against the citizens were not in accord with opinion on this point. The Fourth Republic would take it up again, with a few reservations, and Edgar Faure was to make use of it in December 1955. His adversaries would then denounce the dissolution as a sort of *coup d'Etat*, but their campaign came to an abrupt end: they discovered, in effect, that dissolution was popular. Citizens appreciated having to arbitrate in the political debate, and saw dissolution as a reinforcement of their own power, not as a setback to democracy. Shortly after, moreover, in *La République moderne*, Pierre Mendès France was to advocate government by the legislature.

In agreement on these points, the UF and the UNC were equally in accord in their call for disciplined parliamentary rule: an end to the parliamentary initiative on expenditure, and restriction of the right of amendment, reduction of Senate powers, to prevent it nullifying bills adopted by the Chamber. All these measures of sound sense were to figure in the constitutions of 1946 or 1958.*

There remained the strengthening of the Council's economic and social powers. In this domain the temptations of corporatism were real, but generally avoided. The veterans, including those who belonged to the UNC, had in effect no plans to bestow legislative force on economic and social representation. On this point they were more cautious than those who proposed to turn the Senate into an economic chamber, such as Pierre Mendès France in 1962.

Considerably more moderate than those advanced at the time by men of the right such as Jacques Bardoux, the veterans' propositions suggested an amended and corrected parliamentary régime, not a presidential system. The referendum or increased powers of the president of the Republic as a consequence of the expansion of the body charged with his election, which was suggested by others, were not supported by

---

*Public opinion was upset by government instability, and people thought the citizens had to intervene when the deputies were unable to give permanent support to a government. That was a reason for the broad acceptance of the election of the President of the Republic by universal suffrage in 1962.

the veterans. Faced with an all-too-genuine problem – the impotence of the executive and the ineffectiveness of parliamentary rule – the veterans sought a remedy without stepping outside the framework of representative institutions. It was this path that was to be followed by the elements of 1946 and then, faced with the impotence of the Fourth, by men such as Mendès France. The Fifth Republic was born of their failure.

Notes to Preface to Vichy and the Fourth Republic

1. *La Voix du combattant*, 21 October 1933

2. Henri Pichot, opening speech at the Nice conference, quoted in *Les Combattants avaient raison*, Montluçon, Editions de la Maison du combattant, September 1940, pp.224–25

3. *Le Poilu de la Loire*, 10 March 1932

4. *Les Combattants avaient raison*, pp.140–41

Postscript

This modest book has laid particular emphasis on the political opinions of ex-soldiers, and indeed they provide valuable insights into French attitudes during the inter-war years.

It would however be wrong to conclude from this that the veterans' movement was primarily political: on the contrary, it is precisely its lack of political motivation that makes its value as evidence of public opinion – if the term can have any meaning – so interesting.

The veterans' disappointment at seeing the Third Republic persist in its wanderings thus does not imply that their action was ineffective. The setback of another world war was all the greater because they had worked so hard for peace, but they did not for that reason conclude that they had laboured in vain: their disinterested efforts sufficed to justify them in their own eyes. That their most ambitious objectives were not realised was less significant, in the end, than the day-to-day evidence of camaraderie and mutual help. Activists should not be seen as concerned primarily with international organisation or government reform, for they knew such objectives to be beyond their grasp and public opinion slow to convince. The prime aim of these unsophisticated and tirelessly devoted men was to serve their comrades.

That is why this book ends, in homage to all those obscure participants, with a very ordinary letter which is moving in its simplicity. It was written by a group branch chairman to the doctor in charge of the rehabilitation centre to which he was attached, to say that he was giving up his job in laundry and dry cleaning:

> But although my state of health forces me to leave my job, I shall not give up the chairmanship of the Disabled and Veterans Association. I consider it too fine an undertaking to relinquish and also, as you know, dear Monsieur M—, for anyone with a true veteran's soul in the full meaning of the word it is impossible to abandon the friends who have put all their trust in you.
>
> When I go on visits around the *département* and to national meetings in Paris, and when I see the solidarity that exists between all those who were in the war and the activists of today, I am happy to have been able to do something for the common cause.

Index

Index